Linguistic Pan-Africanism as a Global Future: Reflections on the Language Question in Africa

Vengvengnaa Bonglakyɛre Bɔdɔmɔ
(Adams Bodomo, FGA)

Linguistic Pan-Africanism as a Global Future: Reflections on the Language Question in Africa

University of Vienna, Austria

Inaugural Lecture, Ghana Academy of
Arts and Sciences (GAAS),
Accra, February 10, 2022

GALDA VERLAG 2022

Bibliografische Information der Deutschen Nationalbibliothek
Die Deutsche Nationalbibliothek verzeichnet diese Publikation in der Deutschen
Nationalbibliografie; detaillierte bibliografische Daten sind im Internet über
https://dnb.de abrufbar.

ISBN 978-3-96203-232-6 (Print)
ISBN 978-3-96203-233-3 (E-Book)

TABLE OF CONTENTS

TABLE OF FIGURES

ABSTRACT

Pan-Africanism is a dominant ideological notion in Africa and its diaspora. As a notion, it means that Africa, Africans, and all people of African descent can only stand to gain a better future if the continent and its people unite and pool their resources together politically, economically, and socially. There are therefore different levels of pan-Africanism. These include unity at the political level, with the African Union as the flagship body for ensuring this aspect of pan-Africanism. There is an economic pan-Africanism that encourages the development of more integrated markets and trading zones. The African Continental Free Trade Area (AfCFTA) is a flagship project of economic pan-Africanism. This lecture proposes and analyses the notion of linguistic pan-Africanism as an important aspect of the general notion of pan-Africanism. Linguistic pan-Africanism is the notion that encourages the management of Africa's linguistic resources towards better and more efficient communication and cultural development on the African continent. Without linguistic pan-Africanism, it would be difficult to achieve political, economic, and cultural pan-Africanism. Linguistic pan-Africanism encourages the promotion of major indigenous lingua francas in the different regions of Africa. The ultimate aim may be the creation of a pan-African lingua franca, with a language like Swahili as a strong candidate. Swahili, or Afirihili as some pan-Africanists would like to call it, can be developed as a major global language in the not-too-distant future. The lecture interrogates aspects of these notions with a view to addressing questions such as: how can Africa place itself linguistically to compete economically and culturally? What are the strategies for evolving and implementing effective pan-Africanist language policies to ensure that Africa has a bright global future?

Afu

Afereka-zaa maaloo yɛlɛ (Pan-Africanism) e la yelnyɔgeraa Afereka pɔɔ ane ziiri a Afereka nona nang bebe. O nang e yelnyɔgeraa zung, a tɛgɛ la ka Afereka deme, ane Afereka boorɔ zaa na bang iri la, a nyɛ nendaare maale song ka a paaloo ne o noba lang noɔre teɛ taa ne paati, bɔdi ane lamogerong. Azung Afereka-zaa maaloo yɛlɛ e la tɛɛtɛɛ. Amine la paatiri noɔreyeni ne Afereka Noɔreyeni Lammo (AU) dɛloo, o nang song a Afereka-zaa maaloo. Afercka bɔdi yɛlɛ be la be, a nang dɔrɔ dare landiibu ane yɛrong ziiri. A Afereka deme zaa Yɛrong Weɛ Zie (AfCFTA) e la Afereka-zaa bɔdi bondɛlaa. A mannoo nga teɛre la, a gyɛle Afereka kɔkɔrɛɛ duoruu yɛlɛ nang e tegerong kanga yɛrɛɛ ko Afereka-zaa maaloo. Afereka kɔkɔrɛɛ duoruu e la teɛrong kanga nang na dɔrɔ Afereka kɔkɔrɛɛ lantaa kyaare ne dɛmɛ maaleng diibu, ane yipɔge baabo Afereka paaloo pɔɔ. Ka Afereka kɔkɔrɛɛ kong duori, a na e la tuo ka paati, bɔdi ane Afereka yipɔge nyɛ maaloo. Afereka kɔkɔrɛɛ duoruu dɔrɔ la bamenne yelibe nang e gyamaa, yele Afereka paalong tɛɛtɛɛ. Kaapɔge, a yel-nimizeɛ zaa na la Afereka kɔkɔ-lanna ne kɔkɔrɛɛ, anga Sowahili nang maaleng are soli. Sowahili, bee Aferehili, anga Afereka noba mine nang mang boɔle na bang duori la a waa a donɛɛ kɔkɔsol kanga ka a ba kɔɔre. A mannoo kpegerɛ la a teɛrong na mine, a na iri soorebie anga: wola ka Afereka meng na e de o kɔkɔre ngmɛ ne bɔdi ane yipɔge kyakya? Sobie abuobo la leɛrɛ binnɛ kyaara ne Afereka deme kɔkɔre yeltarre ka Afereka na nyɛ zisong andonɛɛ pɔɔ nandaare kanga?

Nhyɛnmu

Abibiman-nkabom (Pan-Africanism) yɛ adwenemusɛm nnyinasoɔ bi a, agye nhini wɔ Abibiman ne Abibifoɔ a wɔte ammanɔne ntam. Adwene mu no, ɛkyerɛ sɛ Abibiman, Abibifoɔ, ne nnipa nkaeɛ biara a wɔn ase firi Abibiman mu no bɛtumi anya mpontuo ne kankɔ wɔ wɔn asetenam ne daakye a, gye sɛ wɔka wɔn agyapadeɛ ahodoɔ bɔ mu. Wobɛnya weinom wɔ wɔn amanyɛsɛm, sikasɛm, ne wɔn asetena mu ntotoeɛ mu. Wei nti, Abibiman-nkabom gu ahodoɔ pii. Ebi ne nkabom a ɛpue wɔ amanyɛsɛm mu a Abibiman-nkabomu kuo (African Union) ahyɛ aseɛ dada no. Yɛwɔ sikasɛm ntotoeɛ Abibiman-nkabom nso a ɛboa mpontuo wɔ adwadie ne ho nsɛm. Abibiman Asaasepɔn Fahodie Dwadie (The African Continental Free Trade Area (AfCFTA) nso yɛ Abibiman-nkabom sikasɛm dwumadie titire a ɛdi kan. Saa kasakyerɛ yi nam lengwesteks kwan so bɛpɛnsɛmpɛnsɛm, asan asusu Abibiman-nkabom ho na akyerɛ mu sɛ ɛyɛ ade titire a ɛka Abibiman-nkabom ne ne kankɔ ho. Abibiman-nkabom a ɛnam lengwesteks kwan so ne sɛ yɛnam Abibiman kasa ho agyapadeɛ reboa ama amammerɛ akɔ soro na nkitahodie mapa aba Abibiman mu. Sɛ Abibiman-nkabom a ɛnam lengwesteks kwan so nni hɔ a, ɛbɛyɛ den sɛ yɛbɛtumi anya Abibiman-nkabom a ɛfa amanyɛsɛm, sikasɛm, ne asetena mu ntotoeɛ ho. Abibiman-nkabom a ɛnam lengwesteks kwan so boa ma nnipahodoɔ nya kasakoro titire a atwa Abibiman Mantan ahodoɔ ho ahyia no. Ne korakora ne sɛ wei bɛtumi aboa ama yɛayɛ Abibiman-nkabom nnipahodoɔ kasakoro a kasa bi te sɛ Sowahili a ɛbɛtumi ayɛ deɛ ɛbɛdi kan. Yɛbɛtumi ama Sowahili anaa Afirihili a Abibiman-nkabomfoɔ binom frɛ no no anyini abɛyɛ kasa titire a wiase afannan pii bɛtumi ka. Saa kasakyerɛ yi redɔ asukɔ ayi nsɛmmisa yi ano: ɔkwan bɛn na Abibiman bɛfa so akɔ nkan wɔ amanyɛsɛm ne ammammerɛ mu wɔ lengwesteks kwan so? Nhyehyɛeɛ bɛn na yɛde agu hɔ a, ɛbɛboa Abibiman-nkabom kasa nhyehyɛeɛ pa wɔ wiase nyinaa?

Tsakare

Ra'ayin dunƙulewar al'ummar Afirka (*Pan-Africanism*) ya zama wani ra'ayin sanin duniya watau falsafa na haɗin guiwar al'ummar Afirka da 'yan Afirka da ke ƙasashen duniya. A matsayin wani muhimmin ra'ayi, ana ƙoƙarin haɗin kan ƙasashen Afirka da al'ummarsu har ma da 'ya'yansu a fannonin siyasa da tattalin arziki, da zamantakewar al'umma don tabbatar da samun makoma mai haske a nahiyar. Sakamakon haka, akwai fannonin haɗin guiwa a matakai daban-daban don cimma buri, ciki har da haɗin guiwa ta fuskar siyasa, inda ƙungiyar haɗin gwiwa ta Afirka, wato AU take wani hoɓɓasa a yanzu, da haɗin guiwa ta fuskar tattalin arziki. Al'ummar Afirka sun tashi tsaye don gaggauta dunƙulewa ta fuskar kasuwanci da cinikayya na Afrika bai daya, kamar tsarin yin cinikayya maras shinge na AfCFTA da ake tafiyar da shi, wanda ya zama wani muhimmin cigaba ga al'ummar Afirka. A wannan lacca, za a yi nazari game da ra'ayin dunƙulewar ƙasashen Afirka a fannin harshe, wanda yake da ma'ana ta musamman. Ra'ayin haɗin guiwar ƙasashen Afrika a fannin harshe, shi ne zai sa ƙaimi wajen yin amfani da albarkatun harsunan Afirka don ƙara mu'amala da haɗin guiwa da raya al'adun ƙasashen na Afirka. Idan ba a sami dunƙulewar ƙasashen Afirka ta fannin harshe ba, da ƙyar za a cimma burin dunƙulewar ƙasashen na Afirka a fannonin siyasa da tattalin arziki, da al'adu. Ra'ayin dunƙulewar ƙasashen Afirka a fannin harshe shi ne zai bayar da dama a sa ƙaimi wajen yin amfani da harsunan da aka fi yin amfani da su a yankuna daban-daban na Afrika. A ƙarshe dai, za a ƙago wani harshe da za a iya yin amfani da shi, kamar Swahili, ya zama wani babban dan takara daga cikinsu, kamar yadda wasu masu ra'ayin dunƙulewar ƙasashen Afrika suka ambata da Afrohili, inda suke fata wannan harshe zai zama harshen Afirka, kuma zai zama wani muhimmin harshe a ƙasashen duniya nan ba da daɗewa ba. A cikin wannan lacca, za a dubi ra'ayoyin da suka shafi wannan tunani, don lalubo bakin zaren ɗaukaka matsayin harsunan Afrika, don ƙara tsara manufofin dunƙulewar ƙasashen Afrika, ta yadda za a tabbatar da ƙasashen Afirka su samu makoma mai haske.

Muhtasari

Umajumui wa kiafrika ni itikadi kuu barani Afrika na miongoni mwa waafrika waishio ughaibuni. Kama dhana, ina maana kwamba Afrika, waafrika, na watu wote wenye asili ya kiafrika wanaweza kuwa na uhakika kuwa wanapata mustakabali mzuri ikiwa tu kama bara na watu wake wataungana na kuunganisha rasilimali zao pamoja kisiasa, kiuchumi na kijamii. Kwa hivyo kuna viwango tofauti katika dhana ya uafrika (Pan- Africanism). Viwango hivyo ni pamoja na kuwa na umoja katika ngazi ya kisiasa, huku umoja wa kiafrika ukiwa ndicho chombo kikuu chenye kukikamilisha kipengele hiki cha uafrika. Kuna mfumo wa kiuchumi wa kiafrika ambao unahimiza maendeleo ya masoko yatakayounganisha zaidi maeneo ya kibiashara. Eneo la biashara huria ya bara la Afrika (AfCFTA) ni mradi wa kina wa ushirikiano wa kiuchumi wa kiafrika. Mhadhara huu unapendekeza na kuchanganua dhana ya lugha ya kiuafrika(Pan-Africanism) kama kipengele muhimu cha dhana ya (Pan-Africanism) kwa ujumla. Isimu ya kilugha ya Pan-Africanism ni dhana inayohimiza kuunganishwa pamoja kwa rasilimali za kiisimu ya lugha za Afrika ili kujenga mawasiliano bora na yenye ufanisi zaidi na maendeleo ya kitamaduni katika bara la Afrika. Bila uafrika wa kilugha itakuwa vigumu kuufikia uafrika wa kisiasa, kiuchumi na kiutamaduni. Ujuzi wa kiisimu ya lugha ya kiafrika unahimiza ukuzaji wa lugha kuu za kiasili katika maeneo tofauti ya Afrika. Lengo kuu linaweza kuwa kuundwa kwa lugha ya kiafrika-Pan-Afrika, na lugha kama Kiswahili kama hoja yenye nguvu. Kiswahili, au Afirihili kama ambavyo baadhi ya wana-Afrika wangependa kukiita, kinaweza kuendelezwa kama lugha kuu ya kimataifa katika siku za usoni. Mhadhara huu unahoji vipengele vya dhana hizi kwa nia ya kushughulikia maswali kama vile: Afrika inawezaje kujiimarisha yenyewe kiisimu ili kushindana kiuchumi na kiutamaduni? Je, ni mikakati gani inaweza kuendeleza na kutekeleza sera madhubuti za lugha ya kiafrika ili kuhakikisha kuwa Afrika ina mustakabali mzuri kimataifa?

CHAPTER 1

INTRODUCTION

Mr. Chairman, Fellows of the Academy, distinguished listeners, it is an honour for me to deliver this inaugural address to begin my tenure as a Fellow of the prestigious Ghana Academy of Arts and Sciences.

My chosen topic as has been announced is *Linguistic Pan-Africanism as a Global Future*. In this lecture, I make some reflections on the language question in Africa in the 21ˢᵗ Century.

About forty years ago, sometime in 1981 or 1982 when I was an undergraduate student of Linguistics at the University of Ghana, as an avid reader of the People's Daily Graphic, I saw an advert calling for essay submissions to the Ghana Academy of Arts and Sciences (GAAS) on the topic, *A National Language for Ghana*. This means that the language issue has always been an important topic for GAAS. There were to be prizes for the best submissions. I did send in a submission in which I made a passionate argumentation in over 20 pages of a typewritten document on the need to teach many indigenous Ghanaian languages as a basis for evolving a national language with vocabulary input from various Ghanaian languages. There were no computers at the time at Legon, so I cannot retrieve a soft copy of this essay; indeed, I cannot locate even the hard copy in my archives, and I doubt whether it is in the GAAS archives. I suggested that the language to be evolved should be called Gaanakasa, To this day I have never heard back from the Academy and I was even informally informed that the essay competition might not even have taken off for one reason or the other. Of course, as a GAAS Fellow, I intend to help revive this topic of language policy.

So forty years later, today, after knowing my country better than I did as a young undergraduate and after learning more about Africa and teaching it around the world in various places like Europe, North America, and Asia as a professor of African Studies, I want to scale up the Ghana language policy debate to a continental level. The major theme of this lecture is a passionate appeal as I did forty years ago – and as I have always done since then in my numerous publications on this and related topics – for *the promotion and use of indigenous African languages in all sectors of society.* African languages should be used as languages of education, as languages for literary expressions, and as languages in all the institutions of government in Africa. In line with the spirit of this lecture, I now make this clarion call in a selected number of African languages:

"From today onwards I want us to speak African languages everywhere."

Dagaare: A piili zenɛ kyɛ gɛrɛ N booro la ka te yele Afereka deme kokorɛɛ zie zaa.

Akan: ɛfiri ɛnnɛ rekɔ, mepɛ sɛ yɛn nyinaa ara berɛ biara a yɛbɛdi nkutaho wɔ baabiara no, yɛde Afrika kasahoroo no mu biara na ɛdi nkutaho.

Ewe: Tsó egbe dzí héyina lá, medí bé míadó Áfrika-gbewó le te ʄé ɖe síaa ɖe.

Ga: Kɛje ŋmɛnɛ kɛyaa, masumo ni wowie wojaku Afrika shikwɛɛ wiemɔi yɛ he fɛɛ he.

Hausa: Fita ranan yaw, i na son mu ta magana a chiken iyaalaiyan Afrika kooina.

Bambara: Kà bɔ bì, n bɛ à fɛ an ka fàrafinkanw fɔ yɔrɔ bɛɛ la.

Amharic: ከአሁን ጀምሮ በሁሉም ቦታ የአፍሪካ ቋንቋዎችን እንደነገር እፈልጋለሁ። (keahun jemiro be hulum bota yeafrica kankawoch endineger efeligihalehu.)

Arabic: (min من اليوم فصاعدا، فلتحدث بلغاتنا الافريقية في كل مكان alyawm fasaeidan, fel nathdeth beloghatuna alafriqia fi kul makan.)

Swahili: Kuanzia leo nataka tuzungumze lugha za Kiafrika kila mahali.

IsiZulu: Kusukela namhlanje asisebenzise izilwimi zesintu sase Afrika noma kuohi noma nini ngaso sonke isikhathi.

The listener/reader may want to supply the equivalent in their favourite African languages.

Returning to the key terms of the topic itself, we need to understand the concepts of *linguistic pan-Africanism* and *global future* before we begin to discuss the implications of advocating for African languages.

To understand linguistic pan-Africanism we need to first introduce the term *pan-Africanism*. Pan-Africanism is a dominant ideological notion in Africa and its diaspora. It means that Africa, Africans, and all people of African descent can only stand to gain a better future if the continent and its people unite and pool their resources together socio-politically, socio-economically, and socio-culturally.

There are therefore different levels of pan-Africanism. These include unity at the political level, with the African Union as the flagship body for ensuring this aspect of pan-Africanism. We can talk of this as political pan-Africanism, even though the term is hardly used. Political pan-Africanism demands in many ways the knocking down of mostly arbitrary borders imposed on Africa following the Berlin Conference of 1884 (e.g. Mudimbe 1988, Davidson 1994) and thus aiming to remodel a borderless Africa.

There is an economic pan-Africanism that encourages the development of more integrated markets and trading zones. The African Continental Free Trade Area (AfCFTA) is a flagship project of economic pan-Africanism (e.g. Pondi 1987, Sibanda 2021). AfCFTA is a crystallization of the dreams of many Pan-Africanists such as Kwame Nkrumah of Ghana, Sekou Toure of Guinea, Tafawa Balewa of Nigeria, and Julius Nyerere of Tanzania to create a broader economic collaboration for all of Africa (Sibanda 2021).

This lecture proposes and analyses the notion of linguistic pan-Africanism as an important aspect of the general notion of pan-Africanism. Linguistic pan-Africanism is the notion that encourages the management of Africa's linguistic resources towards better and more efficient communication and cultural development on the African continent. Without linguistic pan-

Africanism it would be hard to achieve political, economic, and cultural pan-Africanism.

Linguistic pan-Africanism encourages the promotion of major indigenous lingua franca in the different regions of Africa. The ultimate aim may be the creation of a pan-African lingua franca, with a language like Swahili as a strong candidate. Swahili, or Afrihili (Afirihili is my own preferred spelling)[1], as some pan-Africanists would like to call it (Attobrah 1972), can be developed as a major global language in the not-too-distant future.[2]

Having explained linguistic pan-Africanism, we now turn to the other term in the title of the lecture, global future. The concept of a global future refers to any major worldwide event that can potentially change some systems. Patomaki (2016) describes global futures as referring to on-going and emerging planetary-scale processes, and to their efficacy and real effects, rather than to abstract clock-time. She interrogates: What, then, are the relevant global processes which are open towards the future? Roxburgh et al (2020) talk of global future in terms of how global climatic conservation can be achieved for economic prosperity:

"To reverse nature's decline, and for humanity to enjoy a sustainable and prosperous future, we urgently need transformational change across our economic and financial systems, so they are geared towards delivering long term sustainable development, and the protection and restoration of nature. We need to agree a New Deal for Nature and People to

---

[1] Swahili is also referred to as KiSwahili, so Afirihili can also be referred to as KiAfirihili – the ki- prefix being the noun class marker for 'language' in Swahili and some other Bantu languages. Swahili and KiSwahili are used interchangeably in the literature.

[2] Attobrah (1972) is an early attempt to create a continental language. It is important, however, to note that his idea is a radically different one from what is conceptualised here. Attobrah (1972) aimed for a completely different language, called *Afrihili* not intelligible with Swahili/Kiswahili but my idea of *Afirihili* (note the difference in spelling) is to only supplement existing Swahili/Kiswahili vocabulary with vocabulary items from major African languages. Examples include kente, fufu, akara and ubuntu.

reverse the loss of biodiversity by 2030 and put nature on a path to recovery for the benefit of people and planet".

In this lecture, we want to view language as part of the global ecology that must be preserved. Therefore the claim is that evolving and implementing a cogent linguistic pan-Africanist policy can place Africa in such a strong position that Africa can create tectonic changes in the world, as any global future does. This will ensure that Africa successfully develops its economy and takes its rightful position in the comity of great nations of this world.

The lecture interrogates aspects of these notions with a view to addressing questions such as: how can Africa place itself linguistically to compete economically and culturally? What are the strategies for evolving and implementing effective pan-Africanist language policies to ensure that Africa has a bright global future?

With this basic explanation of the topic of the lecture, I now outline what aspects will be discussed in various sections of the lecture.

In chapter 2, we focus on the literature review, the theoretical underpinnings of the work, and the methodologies used. In chapter 3, we take a closer look at the concept of pan-Africanism, outlining various definitions and types, and ascertaining what it means for Africa to work towards building a unified nation. In the next two chapters (chapters 4 and 5), we focus on outlining and proposing pan-Africanist language policy and language planning at the level of education, at the level of development discourse, and in literary use. We will therefore look at important linguistic debates such as the national language question, the language question in education, and the language question in African literature. In chapter 6, we return to the issue of how Africa can position itself to secure a bright global future if we evolve an effective linguistic pan-Africanism. Africa should not only be concerned about physical natural disasters and how they affect the global economy. Africa should also consider its linguistic and cultural transformation as an important aspect of securing a bright global future for itself. Chapter 7 concludes the lecture.

CHAPTER 2

LITERATURE REVIEW ON THE LANGUAGE QUESTION: THEORETICAL AND METHODOLOGICAL UNDERPINNINGS

In this chapter, we focus on literature review, covering four broad areas: the nature of language and issues of multilingualism, African languages, theoretical aspects of linguistic pan-Africanism, and issues of methodology.

2.1. The Nature of Language and the issue of Multilingualism

Language is not just only a system of communication, of coding and decoding signs. It is an important identity marker. The language we speak defines in many ways who we are; it is one of a person's identity markers along with others such as our skin colour, the clothes we wear, the food we eat, and so on.

Within linguistics and philosophical domains, language is often viewed as an object with which we use to interpret the nature and the world around us, and there is even a strong claim (the Sapir-Whorf Hypothesis (Sapir 1929)) that the structure of one's languages determines the way in which one categorizes and interprets reality. Language is also an important repository of our culture, and is indeed the medium through which we express various aspects of culture in terms of oral literature genres like folktales, folksongs, and dances. Several African philosophers (e.g. Gyekye 1997, Wiredu 1980, 2002) have alluded to the importance of language in the African worldview.

Now, in an ideal monolingual community (and there are hardly any left in the 21st Century), language may be taken for granted since we are dealing with one language without any competing demands for which languages to use in what situation. However, in a multilingual set up, as in the case with all African countries, the language question becomes a prominent issue. Each country, each region of Africa, has a myriad of indigenous African languages, and a substantial number of foreign, non-African languages. African polities are quintessentially multilingual, and a large number of them, especially in Africa south of Sahara still continue to use former colonial languages as official languages and languages of education.

The question then arises as to how to manage this situation. The classical position has mostly been to say that having so many languages in each country is a problem. In fact, multilingualism has been seen as problem, as discussed in Patanayak (1990) for India, and in the case of Africa, it is seen as the basis of ethnic tension since, in much of Africa, language is strongly tied to ethnicity.

There are even more critical voices that blame Africa's problems with achieving rapid development on the linguistic diversity of the continent. Easterly and Levine (1997: 925 - 938), following from Fishman (1966) conclude that there is a correlation between linguistic diversity and economic underdevelopment. According to Easterly and Levine, socio-economic performance is indeed influenced by ethnolinguistic diversity, claiming that the high linguistic diversity of African countries is a dominant indicator of their economic underdevelopment. They pointed out that the economic backwardness of African countries is not only constrained by factors such as "low education penetration, political instability, underdeveloped financial resources, distorted foreign exchange markets, poor management and insufficient infrastructure", but also closely related to a high degree of ethnic-linguistic diversity. If the transition from "complete heterogeneity" to "complete homogeneity" is realized, "productivity increases by 2.5 times and capital per capita increases by nine times" (Easterly and Levine 1997: 925 - 938).

Arcand, Guillaumont, and Guillaumont Jeanneney (2000) reanalyzed and critiqued Easterly and Levine (1997), pointing out that Easterly and Levine had a fallacy in interpreting the data, that in this study, African language status was not "heterogeneous" ", but "multi-polarization", and "multi-polarization" may be a cause of economic growth. At the same time, they also pointed out that the samples of African countries involved in Easterly and Levine's analysis model are relatively limited and unrepresentative, affecting the conclusions' reliability. In the end, they concluded that the data used by Easterly and Levine do not support the assumptions of an African country poverty model, claiming that there is no data to confirm that racial-linguistic heterogeneity is associated with poverty.

Bangura (2000) examines the hypotheses of Fishman (1966) and Easterly and Levine (1997), which both argue that there is a correlation between linguistic diversity and poverty. Bangura investigated research hypotheses on the correlation between "linguistic diversity" and "poverty", changing the terms, linguistic diversity for "multilingualism" and poverty for "economic well-being". Bangura claims that "Colonialism and its later effects" are the underlying reasons behind linguistic diversity and economic poverty (Bangura 2000: 111 – 117). He pointed out that to demonstrate the correlation between language homogeneity and economic development, more diachronic in-depth data is needed as support. His research argues that linguistic diversity can provide "interim solutions to nationalist conflicts" from the perspective of language policy and promote educational development. He concluded that linguistic diversity is an essential positive asset for African countries and can promote socio-economic development (Bangura 2000: 111 – 117).

So the fallacy of linguistic diversity and multilingualism as a problem for ethnic divisions and poverty is the basis for the decision by many countries in Africa to use the "neutral" former colonial language as an official or even national language. The analysis in this lecture discards this position and argues for the benefits of plurality and multilingualism.

2.2. *African Languages*

In this part of the lecture, I highlight some facts about African languages and the language situation in Africa (Bodomo 2017), point to these languages' long tradition in general linguistic studies and their importance in oral literature in Africa.

Language in Africa:

Africa is not only a mineral resource rich continent; it is also a language resource rich continent. Not only are there so many languages on the African continent, Africans also exhibit a very rich multilingual repertoire with many individual Africans in urban centres speaking an average of four to five languages. Indeed, as can be seen in Diagram 1 below, Africa has the second largest number of languages among the continents (Lewis, Simons and Fenning 2009).

There are at least **7,102** living languages in the world.

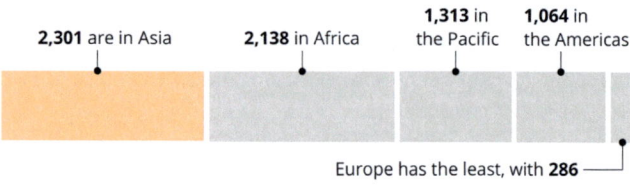

2,301 are in Asia   **2,138** in Africa   **1,313** in the Pacific   **1,064** in the Americas

Europe has the least, with **286**

Sources: Ethnologue: Languages of the World, Eighteenth edition   THE WASHINGTON POST

Diagram 1: Languages of the World

These African languages belong to a diverse set of language families as indicated in diagram 2. It is interesting to know, however, that, with the exception of Arabic, none of the over 2000 languages in Africa are among the top 12 languages of the world in terms of number of speakers, as shown in diagram below:

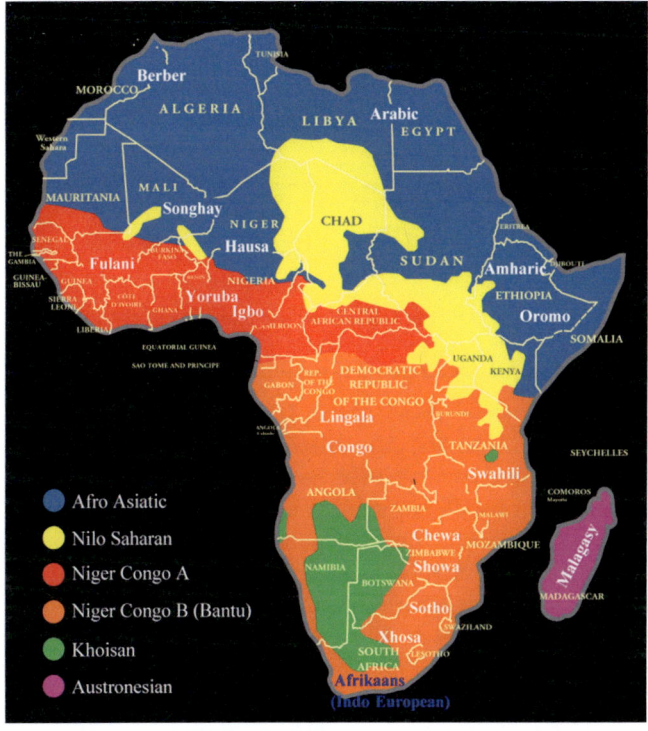

Diagram 2: Language Families in Africa
(Source: http://www.nationsonline.org/oneworld/map/african-language-map.htm)

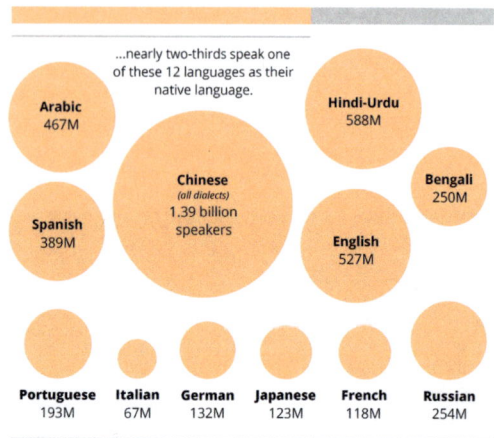

Sources: Ulrich Ammon, University of Düsseldorf, Population Reference Bureau
Note: Totals for languages include bilingual speakers.
THE WASHINGTON POST

Diagram 3: Worldwide native languages

African languages in general linguistic studies:

Whereas the study of African languages has benefited from advances in Linguistics, African languages have also contributed a lot in providing descriptive and theoretical frameworks for analyzing the world's languages, as indicated in Mchombo (1997). Whether in phonetics, phonology, morphology, syntax, semantics, or pragmatics, African languages have provided valuable data for advancing concepts and principles in contemporary linguistic theory.

The click sounds of Khoisan languages (Gerlach 2016) and some Bantu languages like Xhosa and Zulu provided an early discussion and understanding of the concept of phonemes or meaningful sound units. Prior to discovering and understanding the way clicks work in African languages it was not clear that human language has a phonemic inventory for clicks, for whereas click sounds exist in many languages click phonemes do not exist in most languages.

Along with other tone languages, African languages, many of which are tonal, have contributed a lot to our understanding of segments and suprasegments in modern linguistics, leading to the formation of a whole field of linguistics called autosegmental phonology as contained in the works of scholars such as Goldsmith (1990) and Leben (1973).

The concept of double articulation as contained in many African languages, even in their language names, like Igbo and Ewegbe have provided significant interdisciplinary research between phoneticians, physicists, and other speech scientists. The works of linguists like Peter Ladefoged and Ian Madieson (1996) have advanced our understanding of speech synthesis, for instance in the combining of the sound /g/ and /b/ to form /gb/.

In morphosyntax, the rich noun class system of Bantu and other African languages have provided an interdisciplinary framework for collaboration between linguists and computer scientists (e.g. Bresnan 1990, Arvi Hurskanen 2004). Some of the most prominent studies of African language structures and African language situations include Bambgose (1991), Alexander (2008), Asmara Declaration (2000), Fardon and Furniss (1994), Webb and Kembo-Sure (2000), Adegbija (1994), Hendersen (2011), Khan (2014), Mchombo (2017), Nyamnjoh and Shoro (2010), Agyekum (2018), and Phaahla (2010).

The great amount of language diversity on the African continent and elsewhere is of interest to linguists and other scholars who believe in the need for linguistic and cultural diversity, and therefore the need to document and preserve these languages and their associated cultures. This diversity itself is a double-edged sword.

On the one hand, each of these 2138 languages in Africa is the basis of a rich culture as languages are the main media through which we express and convey our cultural values. Major languages from this list are shown in Diagram 4 below[3]:

---

[3]   Rather than making the listing alphabetically, a conscious effort is made to place languages in terms of number of speakers or some sociolinguistic prominence.

West African Languages	Hausa, Yoruba, Igbo, Bambara, Wolof, Akan, Fulfulde, Fon, Dioula, Fula, Moore, Ewe, Ga, Soussou, Malinke, Ibibio, Jola, Mende, Temne, Mina, Kabye
Southern African Languages	isiZulu, Shona, Kimbundu, Oshiwambo, Umbundu, Setswana, Kalanga, Ndebele, Sepedi, Sesotho, siSwati, Tshivenda, Xitsonga, isiXhosa, Bemba, Tonga, Lunda, Chewa, Venda
East African Languages	Swahili, Amharic, Somali, Oromo, Tigrinya, Kikuyu, Kinyarwanda, Kirundi, Luganda, Luo, Kalenjin, Maasai
Central African Languages	Lingala, Kikongo, Banda, Fang
North African Languages	Arabic, Berber (Tamazight), Domari, Tedaga, Amazigh

Diagram 4: Major Indigenous African Languages

These are the five main regions of the continent and their languages, as shown in Diagram 4 – West Africa, Southern Africa, East Africa, Central Africa, and North Africa. The West African region is the basis of the Economic Community of West African States (ECOWAS). It is the most diverse and most populous region of Africa, boasting as many as 16 countries, including Benin, Burkina Faso, Cape Verde, Côte D'Ivoire, Gambia, Ghana, Guinea, Guinea-Bissau, Liberia, Mali, Mauritania, Niger, Nigeria, Senegal, Sierra Leone, and Togo. Southern Africa has an economic community called Southern African Development Community (SADC), comprising the following countries: Angola, Botswana, Eswatini, Lesotho, Mozambique, Namibia, South Africa, Zambia, and Zimbabwe. East Africa comprises countries such as Burundi, Comoros, Djibouti, Eritrea, Ethiopia, Kenya, Madagascar, Malawi,

Mauritius, Réunion, Rwanda, Seychelles, Somalia, Somaliland, South Sudan, Tanzania, and Uganda. Many of these are members of the East African Economic Community. Central African countries include Cameroon, Central African Republic, Chad, Congo Republic – Brazzaville, Democratic Republic of Congo, Equatorial Guinea, Gabon, and São Tomé & Principe. North Africa or the Maghreb includes Algeria, Egypt, Libya, Morocco, Sudan, Tunisia, and Western Sahara. Arabic is the main language here.

On the other hand, the fact that we have many languages within each of the 50-odd polities in Africa means that we face serious challenges and problems for language policy formulation and language planning. The languages themselves as entities are not the problem but there are serious problems in deciding, for instance, which languages to use in our national institutions – in the parliament, in the law courts, in the mass media, and in educational institutions. This scenario has created a language situation in which the languages of the former colonial powers still dominate the linguistic scenes in most countries of Africa, leading to inappropriate terminologies like Anglophone, Francophone, and Lusophone countries of Africa. The truth masked by these terminologies is that we indeed have clearly Afriphone countries in Africa since the vast majority of the population actually speaks African languages as mother tongues and lingua francas. These are languages of wider communication but Africans are rarely permitted to use these languages in formal education, especially at the higher levels, and in some other official settings.

2.3. Theoretical Underpinnings: A Theory of Linguistic Pan-Africanism

The theory of linguistic pan-Africanism espoused in this inaugural lecture has the following underpinnings:

The primacy of indigenous African languages: The most important aspect of the theory of linguistic pan-Africanism espoused here is that all the indigenous languages of Africa are important tools for the socio-economic and socio-cultural development of Africa.

Mother tongue education: Each of these indigenous languages is a mother tongue or language of cultural identity of individuals and various communities in Africa. So indigenous mother tongue education (the need to ensure that all African children can speak, read, and write in at least one of their mother tongues or languages of identity) is an essential feature of the theoretical model of linguistic pan-Africanism outlined here.

Linguistic human rights: linguistic pan-Africanism recognizes that language rights are an essential part of the broader notion of human rights (Grin 2005). The important maxim of *right of language* and *right to language* (Mazrui 2000, Mazrui and Mazrui 1998) in crucial in this model. As Ndhlovu (2008: 138) explains: "[The right of language] is a collective right whose violation automatically affects entire speaking communities. This means that language policies that deliberately seek to suppress some languages would be in violation of the right of language. The right to language is…more of an individual's right to use one or more languages of choice." Mazrui and Mazrui (1998: 115) explains right to language as "the right to use the language one is most proficient in, as well as the right of access to the languages of empowerment and socio-economic advancement."

Linguistic diversity as a global future: Language is an important aspect of our global future. There is therefore a clear link between language preservation and environmental protection. What, for instance, would be the point of preserving all kinds of plant and animal species in a community when we lose the indigenous languages for naming and relating to these plant and animal species? If climatic and environmental sustenance are important global future issues, then language and its preservation are a crucial part of this global future.

2.4. *Methodological Issues*

The research presented here is based on different contexts of research involving a mix of qualitative and quantitative data collection and analysis methods over a life time of observations and reflections on the nature of language and linguistic studies involving African languages. So a lot of archival research has gone into collating various data and ideas. This is also the basis of extensive debates at various conferences and symposia. In some sections, especially in chapter 5, a questionnaire survey was done to capture some opinions and attitudes about African languages.

CHAPTER 3

PAN—AFRICANISM AND THE LANGUAGE QUESTION

This chapter focuses explicitly on connecting the pan-Africanism as mentioned in the preceding chapter to the language question in Africa, Section 3.1 further explains pan-Africanism while section 3.2 builds on section 3.1 by introducing linguistic issues.

3.1. Pan-Africanism

Pan-Africanism is one of the most prominent concepts in the study of Africa and its place in the world. The 'pan' in the term simply means 'all', ie encompassing all Africans and everything Africa. Shepperson (1962) and many other writers suggest that we should distinguish between two types of pan-Africanism on the basis of whether we are dealing with a small 'p' as in "pan" or whether we are dealing with a capital 'P' in "Pan". Hence we have "Pan-Africanism" and "pan-Africanism" (e.g. Nantambu 1998).

Pan-Africanism with a capital "P" would refer to the body of ideas and literature evolved at formal meetings and congresses. In the 20th Century, about five major Pan-African congresses were held in various cities around the world, from Paris in France to Manchester in the United Kingdom. It was at these meetings attended by prominent scholars and political figures from William Du Bois to Kwame Nkrumah that the key tenets of Pan-Africanism were discussed and adopted. I would add the various efforts by African leaders to achieve political unity, leading to the formation of the Organization of African Unity (OAU) in 1963, which later got renamed as the African Union (AU) in 2002.

The other term, 'pan-Africanism' with a small 'p' would then comprise lower level manifestations of unity by people of African descent, both within and outside the African continent. I would add that any time a group of Africans and people of African origins decide to come together to address their interests, they are practising pan-Africanism with a small 'p'.

As has been mentioned in chapter 1, in this lecture, the term pan-Africanism is conceptualised as a notion that propagates unity among Africans. The definition we adopt here is: *Pan-Africanism is an ideological notion that champions the need for Africa, Africans, and all people of African descent to unite and work towards a better future for the continent and for Africans and all people of African descent.*

Of course, the term "Africa" too has to be deconstructed. In my use of the term here, Africa covers the entire landmass of the continent and its islands. We do not make a distinction between the Maghreb and 'sub-Sahara Africa'; in fact, we avoid the term "sub-sahara Africa" altogether. In many European conceptualizations of Africa (e.g. Hegel 1956), there is this keen attempt to distinguish between countries like Egypt, Tunisia, Algeria, Libya, Morocco and the rest of Africa. In the spirit of pan-Africanism, Africa includes all parts of Africa, whether north or south of the Sahara Desert.

So *Africans* in this context refer to citizens and indigenous peoples of all the countries on the African continent and most or all of whom are members of the AU. Africans also include people of African descent who live outside Africa and who trace their ancestry and identity to the African continent. The term 'diaspora' is often used to refer to these people.

In addition to the position we take in this lecture, we will briefly outline other different positions by scholars of pan-Africanism. Pan-Africanism cannot be attributed to one individual as it is a long standing philosophical, political, socio-economic, and socio-culture concept that has been studied and written about by many scholars (e.g. Abdul-Raheem (1996), Anyidoho (1992), Asante and Chanaiwa (1993), Balakrishnan (2016), Bangura (2012), Degesys

(2014), Esedebe (1982), Gyekye (1997), Guevara (2013), Kanneh (1998), Kojo and Chanaiwa (1993), Mudimbe (1988), Mungwini (2017), Mutere (2012), Ndlovu-Garsheni (2015), Nyawalo (2017), Nkrumah (1964), Ouane (2014), Onwudiwe and Ibelema (2002), Prah and Ochwada (2005), Ramose (1999), Sesanti (2017), Shepperson (1962), Simala (2002, 2003), Shivji (2011), Soske (2015), Ugwuanyi (2017), Wa Thiong'o (2004), Walters (1993), Weitberg (2019), Wiredu (1980, 1998, 2002), Womack (2013), Zack-Williams (2016), Weitzberg (2019), Zeleza (2002), and Zizwe (2003).

Of course, in terms of activism some of the major names associated with Pan-Africanism are Marcus Garvey, Kwame Nkrumah, Patrice Lumumba, Amilcar Cabral, Tafawa Balewa, Sekou Toure, Jomo Kenyatta, Julius Nyerere, Haile Selassie, Gamal Abdel Nasser, Ahmed Ben Bella, Robert Mugabe, Samora Machel, Nelson Mandela, Muammar Gaddafi, Thomas Sankara, etc). One of the most important and concise explanations of Pan-Africanism is by Felix (2002: 9) who sees Pan-Africanism as a concept of "…unity in diversity in terms of an extended and expanded African community."

With this explanation of the term Pan-Africanism and its components, we will return to the levels of analysis at the political, economic, and cultural/linguistic levels. We have already looked at political and economic pan-Africanism. Since the subject-matter of this lecture is on linguistic pan-Africanism, we will focus more on it below.

3.2. Linguistic Pan-Africanism

As Simala (2003) has indicated, while there is much lecture on the *language* of pan-Africanism there isn't really much work on linguistic pan-Africanism. The term itself is hardly used and has been actualized in only a few works, including the present lecture. Simala argues that there are two sides to pan-Africanism: "…traditional data (such as race, language, literature, tradition, and territoriality), and egalitarian ideology (such as freedom, equality and fraternity). Pan-Africanism, he argues, is "…a type of nationalism that fused traditional culture and modern ideology to generate the great social power that it [Pan-Africanism] was." Simala 2003: 19). But while a lot has been written about the egalitarian ideology part of it, pan-African linguistic nationalism has not been given the attention it deserves.

In this lecture, linguistic pan-Africanism has been given prominence and, in many parts of the lecture its various elements are elaborated on. We will use the diagram (Diagram 5) below to further outline how we should manage the many languages of Africa from the principles of linguistic pan-Africanism already seen so far:

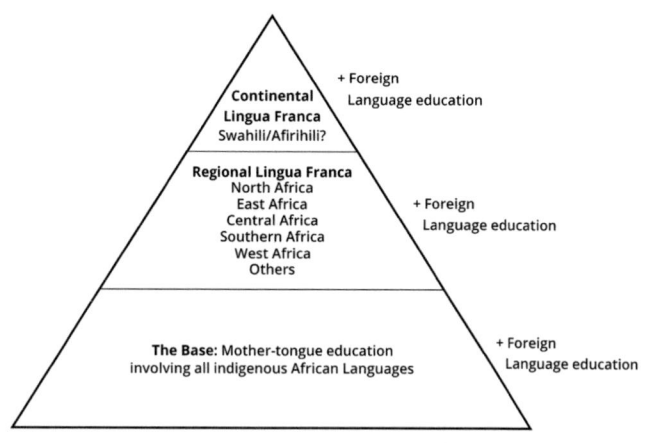

Diagram 5: Diagram for Linguistic Pan-Africanism

The above diagram illustrates all the theoretical underpinnings of linguistic pan-Africanism mentioned in Chapter 2 and elsewhere. The base of the triangle indicates that all African children should be taught to speak, read, and write their mother tongue or at least one of the languages of their cultural identity. The terms 'mother tongue' or 'L1' in themselves can be controversial so I address them in the following.

What is Mother tongue?

At various academic fora, I have often stated that the best language policy for anywhere in Africa is one that ensures that every child is able to be literate (read and write) in their mother tongue, or what linguists sometimes call L1 (first language).

I recognise that these terms are not problem-free. The term 'mother tongue' means "...the language which a person has grown up speaking from early childhood".

Now in my 'mother tongue' or L1, Dagaare, we use the term, tengɛ kɔkɔre. In other African languages like Akan and Hausa it may translate as krom kasa or harshen garina, respectively. Readers should supply terms in their own languages.

So when I use the term 'mother tongue' while speaking English, I am talking of the term tengɛ kɔkɔre and there is little ambiguity in this term.

Now, one of the reasons someone might object to the term 'mother tongue' or L1 is to say that children in the urban centres of Africa grow up speaking many languages, making the term 'mother tongue' or L1 problematic. Yes, it is problematic and one must unpack it. But here are the issues.

First, it is not impossible to have two or more L1s or mother tongues in a multilingual set-up. A 'mother tongue' doesn't always mean mother's tongue. So we can't just throw away the term. In linguistics, unpacking a term doesn't always mean throwing it away unless and until we have a better term. The above clarifications are crucial because these concepts are often the basis of quite a bit of confusion in academic linguistic discussions.

Second, and as a rural African, as someone who grew up in a rural area of Africa, I sometimes get unsettled at how some linguists or other social scientists try to impose what happens in the cities of Africa on all of Africa. One example that was given at an academic forum was that a child in the urban centre like

Nima, a suburb of Accra may grow up speaking Ga, Hausa, Twi, and Ewe at the same time, so which is their mother tongue? The fact that this happens in the cities doesn't mean that it happens throughout Africa. In very many rural areas of Africa (though there is an increasing number of villages along main highways and near cities which may also be multilingual (Sagna and Hantgan 2021)), the term tengɛ kɔkɔre (mother tongue) refers to a specific language and is unmistakable. My tengɛ kɔkɔre (mother tongue) is Dagaare/Dagara, no matter what happens in Nima or Yaba or Sandaga or....where people mash up all kinds of languages, end up with mixed systems and pidgins and don't know who they are, seemingly, in terms of clear linguistic identities.

To complicate the matter further, some Africans in the diaspora growing up in places like America, England, France, Germany, etc, as part of their pan-African nationalism, feel ashamed calling their most proficient languages like English and French their mother tongues or L1, and therefore want to throw away the terms altogether. Well, here is some news for them: you can't avoid the fact that English is your mother tongue because that is what it is. You may deny all you can but you are stuck with it. That is why linguists propose the term 'heritage language'. For children in the African diaspora, your heritage language(s) is (are) your African language(s), probably spoken by your parents to you at home. But English is your mother tongue/L1. Or French, German, Portuguese! If you are a linguist in this kind of diaspora situation of mixed, blurred identity please do NOT impose your own situation on other Africans who have a clear linguistic identity.

Indeed, in my contemporary works, I now also use the term Language of Identity, which is closest to the authentically African terms tengɛ kɔkɔre, krom kasa, marshen garina, etc.

And what does the term "Indigenous African Language" mean?

This is also the right place to address the issue of what an indigenous African language is, since we use the term throughout the lecture and since it is one of the foundation stones of linguistic pan-Africanism. I am often surprised why some linguists question the term "indigenous African languages". The term 'indigenous' is a denotation that simply refers to an entity that originates and occurs naturally in a particular locus, an entity which is native to a particular locality. Any negative connotations of the term 'indigenous' result from a poor understanding of this denotation, and cannot be a reason why we should abandon the term, as Legere (2021) seems to suggest. So we can indeed have indigenous European languages such as English, French, and German, just as we have indigenous African languages such as Akan, Hausa, and Zulu. Is the questioning of the term yet another attempt to prevent Africans from fighting against linguistic imperialism? Indigenous African languages are not hard to recognize from an anti-colonialist perspective: they are those that the former European or other colonialists tried to suppress - and these colonialists then imposed their own languages on the people who speak these indigenous languages. English, French, and Portuguese are not indigenous languages of Africa, but from Akan to Zulu, we see many indigenous languages of Africa. Any language spoken in Africa by communities of people whose original homeland is not traced outside Africa is an indigenous African language. Is this attempt to problematize the term "indigenous African language" a way of trying to place the former colonial languages like English, French, and Portuguese on an equal footing as real African languages - that English, French, Portuguese, Akan, Dagaare, Swahili and Zulu are all African languages? If so this attempt will fail because there is hardly any logical basis for it! English, French, and Portuguese may be languages in Africa but they are not African languages. Africa has its own languages and these are languages that are indigenous to Africa!

So, coming back to the model of linguistic pan-Africanism developed here, the most important step for all governments in Africa is to ensure that all children in Africa learn how to read and write in their tengɛ kɔkɔre/krom kasa/marshen garina (mother tongue/L1), then at least one other language of their country/

Africa. This could be a regional lingua franca for the regions indicated in the middle of the diagram and important candidates include Arabic, Amharic, Zulu, Lingala, Hausa, each representing North, East, Southern, Central, and West respectively. Other important languages in West Africa, which is the most diverse part of Africa, could include Bambara, Wolof, Akan, Ewe, Yoruba, and Igbo.

The apex of the diagram indicates that Africans should agree on a single continental lingua franca, and the best candidate so far is Swahili. So far, it is the most widespread indigenous African language. It is also the most international African language south of the Sahara as it is taught and broadcast in many parts of the world. The African Union could have a policy statement that by the year 2050, ie in the middle of the 21st Century, a modernised form of Swahili called Afirihili or KiAfirihili should become the sole language of the African Union, not just only as a co-official language with foreign languages such as English, French, and Portuguese. It should not only be taught in most universities in Africa, it should indeed be the medium of instruction in at least one university in each of the 55 African countries.[4]

Afirihili must not be thought of only as a linguistic touch-up of Swahili, but as a modernised form of Swahili that develops enough terminologies and concepts for the teaching of African history, culture, traditions, geographies, philosophies, and so on. It would be important for all African children from different

---

[4] Questions may be raised about how feasible this proposal is and whether we can motivate many Africans to sign on to this idea. My response is that the proposal here faces the same or similar challenges that most revolutionary ideas have faced – the risk that this could only be a pipe dream. However, abolishing slavery was seen by many people as a pipe dream until it happened. Independence from colonialism was seen as a pipe dream but it did happen; and the single ECOWAS passport was considered a pipe dream by some people but it did happen. A single indigenous continental lingua franca, which is not synonymous with a single continental language, is not a pipe dream. Africans are motivated to establish a large continental market, AfCFTA. KiAfirihili is a good step towards this goal.

parts of Africa sitting in the same classroom to learn about their traditional African heritages in a common African language, and not in English, French, or Portuguese.

At every level (the base, the meso, and the apex) of the triangle, there is an additional reference to foreign language education which is *outside* the triangle. These foreign languages include the current media of instruction languages such as English, French, and Portuguese in each of the so-called Anglophone, Francophone, and Lusophone African countries, terms we reject in the theoretical model of linguistic pan-Africanism. In fact, this is one of the first times that a language policy proposal for Africa does not accord a central position for Africa's former colonial languages!

It is normal for some bodies in charge of language policy in Africa to continuously interject English, French, and Portuguese (and Spanish because of Equatorial Guinea) into the language policy discourse, thus giving these languages a very large role to play (e.g. OAU 1986, ACALAN 2022). An example of this is the African Academy of Languages (ACALAN), an African Union body in charge of language policy in Africa. In their constitution, for almost every paragraph in which African languages are mentioned, English, French, and Portuguese are also mentioned. The following sentence, for example, can be read at their website:

"ACALAN is entrusted with the task of developing and promoting African languages so that they can be used in all domains of the society in partnership with the languages inherited from colonisation: English, French, Portuguese and Spanish." (https://acalan-au.org/aboutus.php - accessed January 4, 2022)

This is a patently neo-colonial, Eurocentric approach to addressing the language issue in Africa, and must not be allowed to continue. In fact, when the ACALAN is talking of African languages, it refers to a rather nebulous concept: cross-border vehicular languages. Which African languages are not cross-border, and what borders are we even talking about when we want a borderless Africa? And what happens to those languages that are claimed to not be cross-border? Shouldn't we be talking of pooling together all African languages as resources for education? The ACALAN, in my opinion, approaches indigenous African languages in a half-hearted manner and pours all its heart desires unto promoting the former colonial languages. Colonialism can never be a heritage, so describing colonial languages as inherited languages is a fallacy, a misnomer.[5] While a body like ACALAN is needed, for Africa to progress on the language issue ACALAN must be completely overhauled or even have its current constitution or manifesto supplanted altogether! We need a new manifesto of linguistic pan-Africanism!

There is not a single European or Asian or North American country that features African languages in the core aspects of its language policy discourse. Why would any real discourse on how to promote African languages always have English, French, Portuguese and their various pidgin forms as central aspects of the language policy discourse? Shouldn't we begin phasing out English, French, and Portuguese, and any other foreign languages as official languages in Africa?

In our current model, foreign languages, important as they seem to be for some Africans, are kept *outside* the triangle, the main discourse. These foreign languages could include, in addition to English, French, and Portuguese, others such as German, Spanish, Italian, Chinese, Japanese, Hindi. While English, French, and Portuguese, being the neo-colonially imposed official languages, may continue to be used as media of instruction in an interim manner until they are phased out by the year 2050, other foreign languages may be studied at specialist institutions (e.g. Departments of Foreign Languages and Colleges of Translation), since Africans would need experts

---

[5]   Children born from rape do not consider rape as their heritage. Colonialism is rape, and can only be an unfortunate legacy – a negative one as such.

on these languages for Africa's contact with the world. In chapter 6, we discuss how African languages would be developed so that they can compete with foreign languages like English, French, Portuguese, Spanish, German, Chinese, and Japanese for international prominence. As Africa grows more and more important in world issues, especially in matters of demography, it is African languages that we must project onto the world, not the former colonial languages like English, French, and Portuguese. Indeed, a Guardian Newspaper article of January 20, 2022, by Edward Paice, claims that "…a quarter of the world's population would be African…" by 2050. Africa and Africans must reject the neo-colonial notion of going into the world as anglophones, francophones, and lusophones.

With this outline of what may be termed radical linguistic pan-Africanism we now look more closely at how one African country, Ghana, can implement this model of linguistic pan-Africanism.

CHAPTER 4

THE LANGUAGE OF EDUCATION AND DEVELOPMENT DISCOURSE: LOCALIZED ADDITIVE TRILINGUALISM

4.1. Introduction

In their search for solutions to the development problems of Africa, students of African development have often ignored linguistic and other socio-cultural resources (Prah 1993). When linguistic issues are addressed at all, the multiplicity of languages in African countries is often seen as a hindrance to the development of the continent. This lecture focuses on the relationship between language and development and offers a specific proposal for addressing issues of language policy and planning in Africa from the theory of linguistic pan-Africanism established in section 2. Taking the language situation in Ghana as a case study, a pan-Africanist model of development communication and education termed *localized additive trilingualism* is proposed; it is believed to be a model that will enable Africa to harness its multilingual resources for accelerated and sustainable socio-cultural, economic, and technological development in the 21st century.

The theme of this chapter is better highlighted by the story of some young agricultural extension officers and their experiences on one of their first field trips. These young African experts, graduated from one of the universities in Africa, were ready to impart new farming technologies to rural farmers in various areas of their country. On the very first day of the job, they came to terms with one issue which had apparently been neglected in the course of their training: *language*, that most important tool of communication. Despite all the academic theorizing about sharing new technologies with the indigenous people, apparently nobody ever thought that these scholars were going to start working with people, the majority of whom did not communicate in their language of education, in the language in which all the wonderful theories of agricultural extension were propounded.

This story illustrates quite well the cursory attention that, often, language issues have been given in Africa's development discourse. More often than not theories and issues of achieving an accelerated rate of development in Africa are discussed without considering linguistic issues. There are, at least, two reasons for this apparent neglect of the language issue. The first is that development is often conceived of in a rather narrow sense. In an attempt to demonstrate Africa's underdevelopment most people often rush for their calculators and begin to determine GDP, GNP and other economic and financial notions such as income per capita. The consequences of this quantitative approach to development are that economic indicators are often erroneously equated with national development and societal well-being. In this narrow sense then, the role of language in Africa's development may rather be seen as too marginal to be taken seriously.

The other problem why the language issue has not featured well in Africa's development discourse is that the nature and role of language in society is often completely misunderstood. Probably following from the irresponsible declarations of some African writers and intellectuals to the extent that any language can be used to effectively express African culture, an African development economist and educator, who the author talked to, said that African development is language-neutral. He argued that Africa's economic indicators can be bettered just by sheer hard work by Africans speaking whatever language, be it English or French. An allied notion of this general misunderstanding of the role and functions of language is that some people often say that it may even be better to use 'scientific' languages such as English and French since African languages are incapable of expressing certain political notions and all the technical expressions that are inherent in many academic fields.[6]

Refuting all these contentions, this part of the lecture shows that Africa's own languages are central to African development and ought to occupy an important place in the development discourse. We claim that once we liberate the notion of development from the narrow corridors of GDPs, GNPs and the like, and reinterpret it in newer paradigms involving a comprehensive transformation of Africa's socio-cultural, economic, and technological structures, we can begin to appreciate the importance of language in such a transformation.

This interrelationship between language and African development is taken up in Section 1. Following this, we give in Section 2, a synopsis of the language situation in Ghana as an example of the multilingual nature of Africa. Section 3 addresses the challenges of interpreting development in a wider perspective. Issues such as mass participation and local initiative are taken up. It is seen at this point that the present linguistic organization and language policy practices, especially in the educational sector, do not favour our notions of development as mass participation and local initiative, etc. In Section 4 then we propose a new multilingual model of communication in Africa which can facilitate such a view of development. In this model, the centrality of mother-tongue education and of all indigenous African languages is highlighted.

---

[6] Chris Dunton, in an article, *Africa's language problem*, cites Es'kia Mphahlele, an African writer, as saying that he must use English because his mother tongue has no terms for concepts like 'freedom' and 'liberation' (West Africa, March 22-28, 1993).

In this section we shall show that if development is seen as the sustainable socio-cultural, economic, and technological transformation of a society, then language becomes an important variable in the development process (Trudell 2009, 2010); the indigenous language of the society in focus becomes causally related to its development efforts. Indeed, there is a clear link between language and development as conceptualized in the United Nations idea of Sustainable Development Goals (Harding-Esch and Coleman 2017, Marinotti 2016), especially SDG 4 and SDG 16 which deal with providing quality education and promoting peaceful and inclusive societies for sustainable development and justice for all. Recall that one of the theoretical underpinnings of pan-Africanism is right of language and right to language in the socio-economic development process.

What is it that makes language such an important ingredient in the development discourse? The answers must be found in the nature of language and the roles it performs in society.

The Nature and Functions of Language:

There exists a considerable amount of literature on the subject of the role and functions of languages in society. One of the most important elements of the nature of language, probably the most important, – and this is due to the Swiss linguist, Ferdinand de Saussure (1916/1959) – is that language is a system of signs. Languages are similar in the sense that each is a system of signs for encoding meaning and the realities of the world.

However, an important element of language is that it is also culture-specific: each language is systematically different from others in the sense that it has a particular way of arranging the signs that encode meaning, and of communicating the world to its speaker. In that sense then every language is an efficient tool for encoding the peculiarities of the particular environment in which a people live. A particularly strong view of this aspect of language has been articulated by two linguists and philosophers, Edward Sapir and Benjamin Lee Whorf, and has come to be known as the Sapir-Whorf Hypothesis:

> Human beings do not live in the objective world alone, nor alone in the world of social activity as ordinarily understood, but are very much at the mercy of the particular language which has become the medium of expression for their society. It is quite an illusion to imagine that one adjusts to reality essentially without the use of language and that language is merely an incidental means of solving specific problems of communication or reflection. The fact of the matter is that the 'real world' is to a large extent unconsciously built up on the language habits of the group...We see and hear and otherwise experience very largely as we do because the language habits of our community predispose certain choices of interpretation (Sapir 1929).

Since languages relate first and foremost to particular cultures, each individual language seems to represent the speakers of the culture it encodes (Bodomo 2018). This is the basis of the tight relationship between language and ethnicity in many parts of the world. In this sense then language has a symbolic function (Kerswill and Mahama 2019).

From the above realities about language, we see that language is a granary, a repository of the world-view of its speakers, it is this particular language that best contains and expresses the indigenous belief systems – socio-cultural, political, economic and technological - of any society. New belief systems are immediately related to these existing systems. It is in this sense that we notice that the most intelligible and intelligent reactions by speakers to new ideas and technologies are registered through their language.

With this synopsis of the nature and role of language in society let us look at the nature of development and subsequently see how relevant these functions of language are to the development efforts of African countries or any country of the world.

Development as sociocultural transformation:

Development is a contentious concept and this is clearly demonstrated by the multiplicity of approaches within the field of development studies (development as modernization, dependency development, etc.). However, there appears to be some consensus that, development does not just involve the narrow-minded calculation of GDPs, GNPs and per capita incomes, but the complete transformation of the socio-cultural, political and economic belief systems of a particular society to suit its present needs. While the modernization school of development appeals to free free-market forces to achieve this transformation, the dependency school focuses on the factors of dominance and exploitation and appeals to radical steps and state intervention to attempt to eliminate the problems and inequalities in the society in question.

It is in this broader, more comprehensive, view of development that the language factor weighs in heavily on issues of development thinking in every society. We now know that development involves the appropriate transformation of the socio-cultural, political, and economic systems of a society. We also know that language is seen as a repository and a tool for the expression and communication of these very socio-cultural, political, and economic belief systems of the society. Therefore, a successful conceptualization and implementation of this societal transformation can only be achieved through the use of the mother-tongues or the languages indigenous to the society.

Furthermore, we shall see that the language question becomes even more compelling when we look at newer paradigms of development which approach development studies with concepts such as community initiative, indigenous knowledge (Hurskainen

1993) and popular participation. Before we do this, we should ask the question: to what extent has the African development scene approached the interrelationship between language and development as already observed above? An examination of the language situation in some parts of Africa should provide some clues.

4.3. *The Language Situation in Africa*

Current linguistic research continues to strive hard to provide us with a comprehensive picture of the language situation in Africa, which as seen in Chapter 2 is very complex. Still, we do not even have a comprehensive list of the languages spoken in the various countries, let alone to know areas in which they are spoken and how many speakers there are for each language. This is certainly a drawback for research in multilingualism and the subsequent language policies arising from such research. We cannot expect to know the various functions performed by various languages in our multilingual society prior to a detailed linguistic analysis of the languages and their relationships to each other.

Since it is impossible in this context to give a detailed study of the language situation in each African country we wish to do a case study of Ghana, a West African country. This choice is based, not just only on the fact that it is the African country the author knows best, - being a citizen of Ghana – but also on the fact that Ghana is quite representative of the African linguistic situation in many ways.

Case Study: Multilingualism in Ghana

In Ghana, there exist some advances in the attempt to take stock of its repertoire of languages. Kropp-Dakubu (1988), Dolphyne (1988), and Duthie (1988) have undertaken quite detailed analyses of the language situation in Ghana. However, most of these were concentrated in the southern parts of the country. In Bodomo (1994,) these previous efforts are complemented with a quite concise sociolinguistic introduction to northern Ghana and in Bodomo (1996) I arrive at a quite comprehensive list of the indigenous languages of Ghana indicating where each of them is spoken and by how many people. In this section, I shall synthesize information from my previous works and those of others to give the reader a quite detailed picture of the language situation in Ghana.

Indigenous Ghanaian languages:

Ghana's indigenous languages can be categorized into eight major language groups or, more precisely, language subgroups and these are distributed throughout the 16 regions of the country. The term, indigenous language, as used in this lecture is a language whose speakers consider the current location they find themselves in as their traditional homeland and with no known traditional homeland in any other part of the world. I have already defined the term indigenous African languages in Chapter 3. Some of these contain very large numbers of mother-tongue speakers while others hardly number a hundred thousand mother-tongue speakers. However, we do not indicate numbers for the individual languages and dialects because many of the figures are dated, going as far back as the 1960s, which was the last time comprehensive figures were provided in a national census. Below is a presentation of the major groups using their cover name. We also indicate some of the individual languages or dialects under these groups with a rough indication as to their regional distribution in Ghana.

The Akan group:

Dialects/languages under this group include the following: Agona, Akuapem Twi, Akyem, Asante Twi, Brong, Fante, Kwahu, Assin, Twifo, Denkyira, and Wasa.[7] This language group covers the present-day Ashanti, Bono, Bono East, Ahafo, Eastern, Central, and Oti regions. Akan, if it is regarded as one language, is the most widely spoken indigenous language in

---

[7] We should notice that some people still insist that these are languages in their own right and not dialects under any so-called Akan language: we leave that question open here.

Ghana. According to the 1960 population census of Ghana,[8] 2.6 million people spoke the language as a mother-tongue. This made up 39% of the national population of 6.7 million at the time (Dolphyne 1988), divided between the various dialects as follows: Asante Twi, Bron, Akyem, Akwapem Twi, Kwahu, Wasa, Fante, and Agona. There are also many non-native speakers of the language who speak it in various degrees of competence. As mentioned earlier, 1960 was the last time we had reliable figures mentioning the speakers of Ghanaian languages. There have been various attempts to extrapolate these 1960 figures for some of the language groups. The 2021 Census is not really very reliable from linguistic perspectives as the Census did not even attempt to include questionnaires on who speaks what languages.

The Mabia group:

This group, extrapolating from 1960 figures, constitutes 80% of the population of Northern Ghana and approximately 16% of the national population. The 1984 figures by Barker (1986) show that the group as a whole had 1.75 million speakers, making it the second largest linguistic group in the country. The various languages in this group are as follows (Bodomo, Abubakari and Issah (2020): Dagbane, Dagaare - Waale, Gurenne, Kusaal, Mampruli, Kasem, Sisaale, Buli, Konkomba/Likpakpaln, Talni, Birifor, Nanuni, Nabit, Konni, Hanga-Kamara, Bassari, and Moba, Mo-Deg, Tampulma, Vagla, and Chakali[9].

---

[8]   This census was the last in which information on speakers of the various Ghanaian languages was specified. Most other figures about the number of speakers of the various languages are based on extrapolations from the 1960 census. More recent census figures (2010 and 2021) only talked of ethnicities and not languages spoken.

[9]   In response to a query by a reviewer as to why some languages as listed before others, the languages reported to have more speakers and also of more prominent sociolinguistic profiles are listed first. For instance, many of these languages are taught in degree programmes at various tertiary institutions in Ghana. Of course, linguistically they are all important Mabia languages by themselves.

The members of this group cover large areas of the five regions of the North – Northern Region, Savannah Region, Northeast Region, Upper East Region and Upper West Region, concentrating around towns such as Tamale, Damango, Bolga, and Wa, Tumu, Navrongo, Bawku, and Nalerigu.

The Gbe group:

This group is dominated mostly by Ewe within Ghana but there are others such as Fon, Aja and Mina in neighboring Togo and Benin. This language covers most of the Volta and Oti regions, concentrating in the southern parts. Ewe is one of the prominent Ghanaian languages, with native speakers said to number about 1.5 million (Duthie 1988).

The Ga-Dangbe group:

As the cover name implies, this group includes Ga and Dangbe. Dangbe, in turn, includes Ada, Shai and Krobo. This group covers mostly the Greater Accra and part of the Eastern regions. It is quite a sizable group. If we extrapolate from the 1960 census figures Ga may have half a million L1 (i.e. mother-tongue) speakers and Dangbe slightly more than that (Dakubu 1988).

The Guang group:

Members of this group include Gonja, Gichode, Nchumburu, Krachi, Nawuri, Nkonya, Cherepong, Awutu and Effutu. These languages are sparsely distributed around areas in the Northern, Bone, Bono East, Ahafo, Volta, Central and Eastern regions. Gonja is the most prominent in this group, concentrating in towns such as Bole, and Salaga. Awutu-Efutu also concentrates in and around Winneba. In the 1960 census, the total number of Guang speakers was put at 251,810 (Dakubu 1988),

The Nzema group:

This includes Nzema, Sehwi, Anyi (Aowin), Ahanta and Anufo (Chakosi). The last may be mutually unintelligible with the rest, as it is located in a small area of the Northern Region bordering Togo while the rest are in the Western region. Nzema is more prominent in the group, numbering approximately a hundred thousand native speakers in 1960. From the 1960 census, the entire group had 226,920 speakers.

The Buem group:

This group includes dialects and/or languages such as Adele, Lelemi, Bowiri, Sekpele, Siwu, Santrokofi, Logba and Avatime. These languages are found in the northern part of the Volta Region, and also in the Oti regions, concentrating around the town of Jasikan. This is a very small group. Together, they number less than 100,000 based on 1960 population figures.

The Nafaanra group:

This is another small group, probably the smallest. The languages here include Nkuraeng, Nafaanra and Ntrubo-Chala. These hardly number more than fifty thousand native speakers. Barker (1986), estimates that the group in 1984 had 48, 200 speakers. These are found to the western end of the Bono region, bordering Cote d'Ivoire.

Each of the languages above belongs to one of two wider linguistic branches - Mabia or Kwa - which are ultimately members of the Niger-Congo family group of languages.

Other African languages:

In addition to the above languages, there are other West African languages spoken in Ghana such as the Chadic language, Hausa, and some Mande languages (Ligbi and Bisa), whose status as indigenous languages seem to be debatable. While it is true that some of the more "acceptable" indigenous languages spread continuously into Ghana's immediate neighboring countries, where they are also regarded as indigenous, the geographical distribution of Hausa within West Africa, for instance, shows that any Hausa-speaking areas in Ghana would be completely cut off from major Hausa speaking areas such as Northern Nigeria and Niger. This is suggestive of a migration from a clearly identifiable distant area which most speakers of the language regard as their traditional homeland. Further evidence that Hausa may not be indigenous to Ghana lies in the fact that the language is mainly popular in the migrant quarters known as 'zongos'.

English and other Foreign Languages:

Apart from these West African languages which are spoken in Ghana, but which may not be said to be indigenous to the country, though they are indigenous to Africa has a whole, we can name a third group of languages which are clearly non-indigenous to the country. English (along with all its pidgin varieties) is the dominant language in this group but this could include others spoken in very insignificant degrees.

English has been used as an official language since Ghana was colonized by the British and still enjoys an overwhelming position as the language of education and of mass communication vis-a-vis the indigenous Ghanaian languages. English occupies too much space in the schemes of things to the detriment of Ghanaian and other African languages. Though some indigenous languages, especially the government-sponsored ones[10] including Akan, Dagaare, Dagbane, Dangbe, Ewe, Ga, Gonja, Kasem and Nzema are beginning to challenge this position in their respective regions (such as on FM radio and in other mass media)[11],

---

[10] These are languages selected by government for the purpose of publishing educational material in them through its language bureau, the Bureau of Ghana languages. This, to me, is about the nearest thing to the idea of selecting some of the main languages of the country as national languages, as is the case in some other African countries such as Nigeria and South Africa.

[11] Many of these languages such as Akan, Ewe, Ga, Dagaare, Dagbane, and Nzema are also taught in schools and tertiary institutions and are also included in the West African Examinations curricula at Senior High School levels.

English is still very widely used in the country if we consider all its forms – from pidgin to standard educated English. Of course, this situation has come about because of an interplay of historical, linguistic, educational, and political factors, factors that any pro-pan Africanist language policies must address.

Other European and foreign languages include French (taught as a school subject and spoken among educated bilinguals) and Arabic (taught in Islamic schools known as 'makaranta' and spoken in Lebanese communities).

Summary:

The above case study confirms that African societies are highly multilingual and that Africans themselves are rather polyglotic, using their mother tongue in their immediate local environment, and any other inter-ethnic languages and lingua francas once they leave their environment. Indigenous African languages are still vibrant and widely used by the vast majority of the population. Unfortunately, however, these indigenous languages – important means of communication in African societies – are not widely used in the formal educational systems. These same languages are not the languages of the national government, and the languages of mass communication are hardly the languages of the people. As an example, in Ghana as much as 51% of the total amount of annual broadcast hours is reserved for English alone, leaving the rest for all the many Ghanaian and African languages.[12] This scenario has however been challenged with the introduction of many local FM radios and TV stations that promote the use of many of these indigenous languages. This situation then confirms our contention that there is a linguistic and communicative discrepancy on the African continent and has non-trivial consequences on the socio-political, socio-economic and socio-cultural development efforts of the people of Africa.

---

[12] Source: Ghana in Figures 1992. Statistical Services. P.O. Box 1098, Accra.

4.4. Problems for New Approaches to Development

Given the fact that three or more decades of development theorizing seemed to have brought nothing but hardship on Africans, various initiatives are underway (e.g. UN-NADAF document) to redefine the concept as it pertains to Africans.[13] Newer paradigms of development studies have come up in recent fora on development discourse (Akin Aina 1993; von Troil (ed.) 1993, etc.).

Most of these newer paradigms seem to have certain things in common. All seem to put indigenous African peoples at the centre of the development process. As a result issues such as mass participation, community initiative, the democratization of development (UN-NADAF document) and indigenous knowledge (Hurskainen 1993) come to the forefront.

The above linguistic situation in Africa creates some problems for these newer approaches to development in Africa. For how could we harness indigenous knowledge, how could we generate local initiative and mass participation in the development discourse if the elite in Africa continues to use languages that are not the languages of the indigenous people? Prah (1993: 50) puts things in perspective with the following:

> The dilemma in Africa with regard to language and development is that...the elite which is entrusted with the leadership in the development endeavor is created in, and trapped by the culture of western society, and favors the reproduction of entire western images in African development. The elite in effect sees Africa from outside, in the language, idiom, image, and experience of the outsider, in as far as the African mind is concerned. It is unable to relate its knowledge to the realities of African

---

[13] UN-NADAF stands for United Nations New Agenda for the Development of Africa in the 1990s.

society. It is estranged from the culture of the masses, but realizes almost as an afterthought, that development as a simple replication of the western experience is 'mission impossible'.

What is clear from the above is that if Africa does not have to revise its newest approaches to development within a very short time again, then the language question must be causally tied to African development thinking. The realization that development can only be possible with the massive involvement of Africans themselves and not just only the elite puts the indigenous languages right at the centre of this development discourse. This is a strong basis for our appeal to practitioners within the field of development studies to evolve a language paradigm for development to be known as Development Linguistics.[14] If development is seen as harnessing the indigenous knowledge and initiative of Africans then the most effective language of development in Africa cannot be the former colonial languages, languages of the rulers, of the elite. It has to be the languages of the people of Africa, languages in which we expect to find the most intelligible and intelligent reactions from the African peoples who are the agents of development.

If this view is agreed upon by all, then it behooves Africans to put in place a language policy that would achieve these development goals and aspirations. In the next section, based on a careful observation of the synchronic features of African society, a model of development communication for Africans termed localized additive trilingualism is proposed. We believe that this model – which may be regarded as a linguistic pan-

---

[14] This term should be distinguished from developmental linguistics which deals, among others, with child language acquisition and learning. Development Linguistics, like other fields of Development Studies, such as Development Economics, Development Education and Development Geography, may be concerned with how to apply linguistic and sociolinguistic theory to the development of the developing world.

African model – can serve as an important development strategy if well implemented.

4.5. Towards a Pan-African Model of Localized Additive Trilingualism

I propose a multilingual communication model which will emphasize the use of the mother tongue and other indigenous African languages at various levels of social organization. It is a model which will make it possible to accommodate most, if not all, of Africa's languages, using them as essential tools of communication for development, irrespective of their numbers of speakers.

The three-way Categorization of Society:

It seems that society in many countries of the world including those of Africa is organized broadly in a three-way structure: The figure below is meant to be a partial model of this social structure. It includes various political, administrative and educational levels and their linkages, together with the linguistic entities that are or ought to be used at each level.

At the political-administrative level, from an African perspective, we seem to have national, regional and a continental level of administrative entities. In Africa, we have the various countries (55 of them), then regional entities like ECOWAS and SADC. And of course continental level entities like the AU and AfCFTA. Each of these may have sub-divisions. The Ghanaian political-administrative structure may be used to illustrate this social organization. Most, if not all, state institutions have three levels of operation: the national, the regional and the district; and this is evidenced by the fact that each such organization would have a national office, a regional office, and a district office. Even at the level of government, there is the national parliament, but also new innovations are being made in the political structure, in which we have the important notions of regional consultative councils, and more importantly, district councils. Elections are held at both national and district levels and appointments made at the regional levels.

Educational structure:

The same-three way societal organization can be observed in the educational systems of most countries of the world. There is a hierarchical structure of primary, secondary and tertiary educational organization in most countries of Africa, with very minor different internal subdivisions. In Ghana, the educational system comprises 6 years of primary education, 6 years of secondary education, divided into junior and senior secondary schools, and finally leading to a tertiary level of education. At each of these levels we have different participants, interest groups, administrators, teachers, educational resources, and goals of education.

It seems to us then that each of these levels constitutes an important level at which communication takes place, at which participation and decision-making by the citizenry takes or ought to take place. The district, the regional and the national constitute discrete and important development cells of any country.

Ingredients for a model of localized additive trilingualism:

What important lessons does this observation of the society present us in the language debate? It is clear to us that it is desirable for multilingual countries to formulate language policies which would seek to exploit this natural model of social organization to achieve optimal communication among the citizenry at each level. We believe that the best language policy is one that can promote communication between discourse participants at each of these levels and between each immediate level in multilingual set-ups. In short, we observe here that language policy must have a strong interrelationship with social organization.

In addition, we formulate the principle of the most appropriate language of development in the African set up: for effective development communication in each social set up, the most appropriate language must be used in both spoken and written discourses. These principles derived from the theoretical model of linguistic pan-Africanism developed earlier: right of language and right to language, seeing multilingualism as a resource and not a hindrance to development, etc.

Development communication is any communication between participants for the purpose of sustainable socio-cultural transformation. By most appropriate language we mean the language in which the majority of participants in any discourse entity have communicative competence. With the above ingredients, we then move ahead in the next section to formulate and illustrate a model of development communication for African countries, which we term localized trilingualism.

Localized Additive Trilingual Model for African Development

We begin by recognizing the fact that the African society is broad and diverse; as such, it is difficult to develop a linguistic model for the whole of Africa. We do believe however that there are enough similarities in Africa's historical experiences and socio-linguistic organization to permit some reasonable amount of generalization. Characteristically, most, if not all, of Africa has experienced foreign invasion and power domination with the result that the colonial or the dominant powers have superimposed their languages over already existing indigenous languages. The introduction of these new languages of power has not only increased the multilingual repertoire but has created situations in which attempts have been made to suppress the indigenous languages altogether or, at least, relegate them to the confines of the informal sectors of each country. This diglossic picture, where the foreign colonial languages are reserved for the formal sectors and the indigenous languages or pidgins the informal, is quite representative of the African linguistic scene.

Recognizing the diversity and sociolinguistic peculiarities of each African country, our model does not attempt to specify a particular and specific language policy for all African countries. What it does is to address the above general diglossic situation and to propose the promotion of the use of Africa's indigenous languages in all sectors and levels of the social organization.

The model proposed is referred to as localized trilingualism (Bodomo 1995, 1997), now referred to as localized additive trilingualism because:

i. the average citizen who has gone through basic education should be functionally competent in spoken and written discourse in at least three languages. Ideally, most citizens should be trilingual in Africa, obtaining competence in their mother-tongues, in a wider regional African lingua franca and in a language of global communication such as Swahili (and some former colonial languages including English and French).

The issue of the trilingualism being additive is stressed here because in colonial setups, what obtained was subtractive trilingualism. For example, the child is taught English through their African mother tongue with the aim of using English in most domains while restricting the mother tongue to informal domains. In the current model, we emphasize additive trilingualism – where the process ends in more or less equally competent levels of literacy for all three languages.

ii. the trilingualism will be different from community to community, with differing mother tongues at the national levels but more and more similar languages at regional and continental levels.

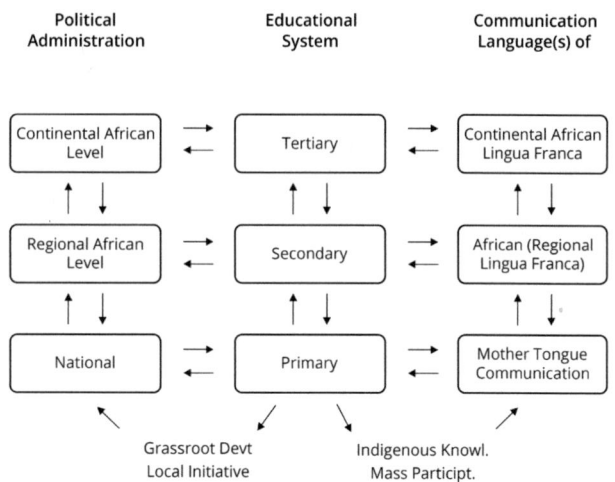

Diagram 6: Localized Additive Triangualism: A Model of Linguistic Pan Africanism

From the diagram this should be the progression in language acquisition and learning:

Primary/national level	Mother tongue
Secondary/African regional level	Mother tongue + regional African lingua franca
Tertiary/Continental	Mother tongue + lingua franca + continental African language (most likely, Swahili/Afirihili)

It may sometimes happen that the mother-tongue is the same as the regional lingua franca. In that case then another African language within the region should be learnt.[15] Having given a

---

[15] In the 1970s, the Ghanaian government had a program which, at least, in rhetoric, encouraged every citizen to learn how to speak another Ghanaian language.

broad picture of the model we now move ahead to consider each level of the social structure.

On Language and Development

The National/primary level

Based on our principle of most appropriate language, we believe that the most appropriate language for the development discourse at the national administrative level (ie within each African country) and the primary school level is the mother tongue. Since our (formal) model defines most appropriate language as one in which the majority of participants in any discourse entity have communicative competence, the mother tongue is the language most people use at this level. In many parts of African countries the primary schools situated in them are usually – but not always – linguistically homogenous entities and the resource persons in such areas – the administrators, the teachers, etc. – are invariably drawn from the cultural area. Village meetings for community self-help projects can best be conducted in the mother-tongues. Primary school children are already orally very competent in their mother-tongue and will therefore learn linguistic abilities such as reading and writing faster. Concepts in mathematics and science presented in the mother-tongue would be more easily grasped than if they were taught in a different language. The use of the mother tongue here will enable the children, future leaders of the community, to competently grasp the belief and knowledge systems of the society. This is based on the fact mentioned in section 1 that language is a receptacle, a granary of the indigenous knowledge systems of the community.

On the other hand, the use of the mother-tongue at all institutions situated in the district – schools, offices, district parliament and other community gatherings – will enable the chiefs and people of the community, today's resource persons for grass-root development, achieve maximum participation in terms of the ideas and information they receive and provide.

They will be able to react to new ideas in the most intelligent ways possible.

From the diagram, it may be observed that it is at the primary/national level that we find newer ideas and approaches to development, such as local initiative, mass participation and grass-root development. The mother tongue is intimately tied to this level of the social structure and ought to be the most appropriate tool for achieving the development goals of the particular society.

Our intimation then is that there should be an uncompromising institution of the local language of the community in all areas of human activities. An important goal of the educational system at this level should be to ensure that primary school graduates are well-grounded in the mother tongue and can use it to speak and write about any grade level theme, be it in literature, mathematics or science. Workers coming into this district and who do not already have competence in this language should be given proficiency courses in the language so that they serve the indigenes of the society more competently.[16]

The question has come many times as to how mother tongue education can be achieved in more heterogeneous sections, such as in urban centres. Our response is that more than half of Africa is still in the rural set up where there is more homogeneity. We claim, however, that while the choice is difficult in urban centres, the model can respond to it adequately and the answer should not be to teach English or French or any of the former colonial language as the case may be, but to undertake a sociolinguistic

---

[16] Many people, including a reviewer for this publication, often raise the issue of cost, funding, logistics and so on. The question is often asked: 'where do we get money for mother tongue education in areas such as getting trainers of language instructors and developing teaching materials'? My response is that if we can do the same thing for our former colonial languages like English and French, we can equally do that for our African languages, if there is the motivation, Indeed, it may even be less costly to set up African language programmes than foreign language programmes.

study of the classes and the most appropriate language here chosen. This would most likely be the lingua franca of the area, a language in which most of the children have near mother-tongue competence. For instance, in urban centers like Accra and Kumasi, the most appropriate language in most schools may not be English but Ga or Akan. While the situation may be a bit tricky in urban and cosmopolitan centers, mother-tongue or near mother-tongue education and societal use can still be achieved, based on the principles and assumptions of our model of linguistic pan Africanism.

The African regional/ secondary level:

For effective development discourse to take place at the African regional level such as ECOWAS, SADC, etc., as the case may be, it is our contention that the most appropriate language be encouraged and used as the medium of communication at political and administrative institutions. In the educational sector, this most appropriate language which would most likely be the lingua franca of the region should be the main language of instruction at secondary level institutions. A student graduating with the General Certificate of Education, if he or she is to be useful to his or her region and to the vast majority of indigenous people in that region, should be competently literate in the language spoken by the vast majority of the people of the region. As a future agent of technology transfer, of general development, the high school graduate must be able to carry out a sustained spoken and written communication on issues from his or her chosen field – arts, science, or technology – in this major African language of the region.

I propose the following as regional African languages in each of North, East, Central, Southern, and West Africa:

North/Magreb: Arabic
East Africa: Swahili and Amharic
Central Africa: Lingala

Southern Africa:	Zulu and Shona
West Africa:	Hausa, Akan, Bambara, Moore, and Wolof

Criteria for selection of regional African languages should include the fact that at least 20% of the population of the region should speak the selected language. This choice must be based on an elaborate sociolinguistic and population census data. Secondly, there should not be more than five languages in each region, and no one country in the region should have more than one language represented.

The continental/tertiary level: a reality of afriphone Africa

Choosing a single indigenous language as medium of communication at the national level has been elusive for most African countries, let alone a single lingua franca for all of Africa. As has been mentioned above, apart from the linguistic multiplicity in these countries, there are many major regional languages, all of which are competing candidates, and it is obviously difficult to settle on any one of them, without causing some discontent among sections of the population that may lead to conflict (see Laitin 1994 for Ghana).

The easier solution, if it may be said to be any solution at all, has mostly been to agree on the former colonial language as the official language. This is the basis of the linguistically false terminologies we often hear about African countries: African countries which are more appropriately called afriphone are divided in to 'anglophone', 'francophone' or 'lusophone'. It is my contention that until we revise this fallacy of referring to afriphone countries as europhone we can never come to a real and deep understanding of the linguistic realities of our continent. The term 'anglophone' used to describe a country like Ghana, for instance, masks the reality that more than 90% of Ghanaians use African languages in their day to day activities. It is only about 10% of the elite, dominating academic and political administrative institutions, who use European languages profusely in their day-to-day affairs. Consequently, they are the ones who find it expedient to refer to afriphone countries as 'anglophone', 'francophone' or 'lusophone'.

We believe therefore that Africans must make a bold decision and agree on one major African language as the overall lingua franca for all Africans in Africa and Africans in the diaspora. Any of the regional languages mentioned above could be good candidates but realistically the most widely spoken and studied language in Africa is Swahili. Swahili should be the overarching continental lingua franca.[17]

Swahili must be curated and made to serve as continental lingua franca. One way to do it is to enrich the current vocabulary of Swahili with vocabulary from major African languages, such that speakers of each major African language can feel a sense of their language having contributed to the new African lingua franca. At least one pan-Africanist has made an attempt in this wise (Attobrah 1972) and called the language Afirihili. However, what is produced is a totally different language. Our proposal would be to slightly enrich the language at the level of vocabulary and leave Swahili grammar intact. The new, curated pan –African lingua franca would be called Afirihili (note the difference in spelling).

It is time for Africa to remove the former colonial, European languages as official languages and replace this with Afirihili and the regional lingua franca. European countries never consider African languages in their language policies. Why should Africans continue to include English, French, and Portuguese as official

---

[17] While this is certainly a robust, ambitious proposal, it is not overambitious! No other African language has the same level of acceptability at the continental and even at the regional levels as Swahili. It is the most widely studied African language outside Africa, and in African universities. If pan-Africanism is seen as overambitious, then linguistic pan-Africanism, especially the Swahili aspect, cannot escape the charge of being overambitious. However, pan-Africanism has ambitiously resulted in relatively stable institutions like the AU and AfCFTA. In the same vein the rise of a continental lingua franca will be a stable reality.

languages of Africa? In the same way that other parts of the world like Europe, Asia, and North America have specialist programmes for studying foreign languages, Africans can also continue to offer foreign languages like English, French, Portuguese, Chinese, and Japanese in scholar curricula, but not as official languages. Of course, European languages may continue to perform limited roles in the country as languages of diplomacy and of contact with the outside world. Africa must evolve a unitary lingua franca, Afirihili, by the year 2070.

Our model responds to all these by featuring an African language and the former colonial language (English, French, etc.) at this level. As a transitional process, these and anyone or two African languages may be used concurrently in all national institutions and at the tertiary levels. This arrangement would be easier for certain countries such as in East Africa, with the spread of one main lingua franca, Swahili, but may be a bit more challenging in some West African and Southern African countries.

The Linkages:

Our model diagram indicates connecting arrows between the various levels of our three-way social organization: the national-primary, the regional-secondary and the continental-tertiary. These are supposed to represent transition points, points at which participants and realities at these levels interface and influence each other. For instance, in each country, it is district administrative level personnel that influence decisions at the first educational cycle more than the other levels.

From a linguistic perspective, one has to consider, for instance, how to move from the mother-tongue medium of instruction to the regional and finally to the continental language, Afirihili. One solution at the primary level would be to teach the regional language as a strong school subject in anticipation of using it as a medium of instruction in the second cycle institutions. At the second cycle institutions, one must start teaching Afirihili as a strong school subject. The concept of a strong school subject implies giving the student proficiency lessons in the language for at least one hour daily.

4.6. Conclusion

This chapter has discussed a new linguistic pan-Africanist strategy – a strategy which draws attention to the language issue in the development discourse of Africa. Africa seems to have had more than its fair share of the global political, economic, and social instability. Five decades of attempts at continental development and prosperity since the attainment of independence still leave the continent with mostly bleak economic and political statistics. Faced with this state of affairs, newer paradigms of development have been sought for Africa (e.g., UN-NADAF). Central to these newer paradigms are concepts such as mass participation, local initiative, indigenous knowledge, etc. But the language issue has hardly been taken seriously, even in these newer paradigms.

It has been the contention of the paper that the aims and goals contained in these concepts which draw attention to the role of indigenous Africans themselves in the development discourse can never be achieved without serious considerations of the role of African languages. The point is that there is an important language paradigm in African development. It was this same point that the Dutch psychiatrist Hilbert Kuik aptly expressed, and which has stayed largely ignored by students of African development:

> When people speak of developing countries, they immediately think of economic backwardness. To deal with that, projects are conceived and technicians and money sent. When the projects fail, blame is put on the social and cultural practices of the people...Only rarely do people (from the donor countries) realize that the language barrier is the

culprit which prevents new ideas from taking root...
the fact that the inherited colonial official languages,
French and English operate more as inhibiting than
facilitating factors, is a point which in my estimation
is poorly appreciated by both the local governmental
authorities and the international agencies (quoted
from Prah 1993).

It is only when new ideas are communicated, when
technology transfer is done, in the indigenous African languages
that Africans can begin to get nearer an increased participation in
the development discourse.

All these points were argued for by drawing on facts about
the nature and functions of language as a tool for communication
and as a vehicle, store, and receptacle of indigenous and new
knowledge. Development was reinterpreted as a comprehensive
socio-cultural transformation which needed massive participation
of the indigenous people as agents of change.

But an examination of the African linguistic situation, based
on a case study of Ghana, indicated clearly that there was a
linguistic discrepancy: the language of government is not the
language of the governed, the language at the district level did
not feature much in the development decisions.

To redress this discrepancy, a model of linguistic pan
Africanism - a development linguistic strategy - we termed
localized trilingualism (Bodomo 1995), relabelled localized
additive trilingualism (in the paper) has been developed. In this
model, the mother-tongue is to be widely used in the district
institutions such as local political assemblies and first cycle
institutions as a medium of communication and education.
Another African language is introduced at the regional level and
Afirihili is introduced at the tertiary level.

One objection might be that a three language model is too
cumbersome. But this criticism would not stand when we realize
that Africans by nature are already very polyglotic and their

society very multilingual. Africans naturally and voluntarily learn newer languages as they move further and further away from their districts in the rural set-ups to the national level. This model is based on and motivated partly by this linguistic flexibility on the part of the majority of Africans. Rather than being a hindrance to national development, polyglotism, multilingualism and the attendant multiculturalism are resources (Baugh 1994, Rickford 1995) that can be harnessed for the development of Africa. The language issue is highly crucial in African development discourse. The need for an accelerated development should be enough motivation for Africa's politicians and educational authorities to make the resources available for an effective implementation of this language policy proposal.[18]

---

[18] This section of the lecture is based on research undertaken at Stanford's School of Education program of Language, Literacy and Culture in the 1994/95 academic year. I thank Professors John Baugh, John Rickford, Melanie Sperling, Sugie Goen and several participants of the literacy seminars for various discussions on my work. I thank participants at various seminars on Stanford campus where preliminary versions were read. In particular, I thank John Mugane, for constant discussions. I am also grateful to several people in Scandinavia, especially Assibi Amidu and Arvi Hurskainen, editor of the Nordic Journal of African Studies where an earlier version appeared, for several comments that improved the study.

CHAPTER 5

THE LANGUAGE QUESTION IN AFRICAN LITERATURE: AFRIPHONE LITERATURE

In this section of the lecture, we extend reflections on the language question in Africa to African literature. A long-standing debate within African literature and indeed in much of Africa's linguistic expressive discourse is whether it is best to use African languages or the former colonial European languages in African literary writing and general academic discourse. More specific questions include the following: Are English, French, and other foreign languages appropriate for African literature? Can we still refer to a piece of work as African literature if it is not written in an African language? Two major positions, each representing either side of the debate, are often advanced. One position claims that African languages are central to African literary expressions and should be the ones we should naturally use for writing and encoding African literature. The other says that, given our colonial past which has led to much European language literacy education and given Africa's complex multilingual situation, we are better off using the former colonial languages English, French, and Portuguese in producing African literature. There are, however, minor positions that try to reconcile the two major positions and suggest that this should not be an 'either…or' issue but a 'both' issue. However, more questions still remain beyond attempts to reconcile the two major positions in the debate. This section of the lecture carefully looks at either side of the debate before making some proposals that draw in insights from linguistics and cognitive science to suggest ways in which we can align the plethora of languages used in Africa to understand what African literature is or ought to be (Bodomo 2016).

In so doing, we demonstrate in this chapter the importance of the language we use in literary productions around the world. We argue for the idea that the best and most realistic way for African literature to contribute to a body or collection of world literature is to use African languages to create literature that expresses African cultures and thought systems. This is termed Afriphone literature.

5.1. The Language Question

To begin to tackle the debate surrounding the question of what language to use in African literature we need to decide for ourselves what African literature is or should be in the first place.

What is African literature?

Literature has many definitions and conceptualizations but it usually involves a form of artistic creation by an individual or group of individuals with language (written or spoken) that attempts to represent some conceptualization of a possible world, real or imagined. We will now put forward a working definition and gradually modify it in account of our discussions until we conclude the chapter with a more definitive definition.

i. African literature then would presumably be literature as defined above that is created by an African (as opposed to a non-African) to represent some aspect of the African world, real or imagined.

The difficulty created in the above definition would lie with establishing who an African is and what this African world is.

As a result, we need to revise the definition to address these problems.[19]

---

[19] Many preliminary definitions are advanced before reaching the final one. This is intended as a discursive approach that gradually convinces the reader to abandon the notion of 'Anglophone/Francophone African literature' and warm up to the notion of Afriphone literature.

ii. African literature is a form of artistic creation produced in the medium of language (written or spoken) by an artist or group of artists with African experiences to represent some aspect of the African world.

This basic definition can be extended to specify what language is used and what we mean by African world. We do not need to belabour the issue of who an African is because we are not requiring the artist to be a citizen of any of the countries on the African continent or even be born there. We require them to have African experiences of significant degree, meaning to have experienced and understood some socio-cultural aspects of the African world in order to be able to express and represent them artistically.

What we need to specify are the issue of 'language', the very subject matter of our discussion here, and the issue of 'African world'. We will be non-committal about language in the current *working definition* and at the end of the chapter we will then decide how to specify this. We will also try to extend the issue of "African world" to mean the landscape of the continental landmass of Africa and all the cultures represented on this landmass and its associated islands along with diasporic exportations of the cultures of the continental landmass.

iii. African literature is a form of artistic creation produced in the medium of any natural language (written or spoken) by an artist or group of artists with substantial enough experiences of the landscape of the continental landmass of Africa and its associated islands, along with diasporic exportations of the cultures of this continental landmass.

It should be easy to delineate this continental landmass because it is neutral in terms of geographical reality with clear enough sea and land boundaries. It doesn't say anything about nations or people because every group of people living on the African continent is subsumed under this definition, unless of course they want to opt out, in which case it would then be a personal or group identity *exceptionalism* to which they are entitled.

There are, at least, two things we can do to this definition. Make a catalogue of any group of literary artistic creations and then try to see if we can include or exclude them as African literature on the basis of this definition. Consider the literary works: *Things Fall Apart* by Chinua Achebe, *Une Si Longue Letter* by Mariama Ba, and *Heart of Darkness* by Joseph Conrad. Variable parameters will include the origins and identity of the writer (what are the citizenship, gender, cultural background of the author), and setting of the work of art (is it mainly on the African continent?). Others are themes of the work of art (is it expressing some aspect of the society or culture of the African geographical landmass?), and language (what language is used, is it indigenous to the African continent?). The subsequent sections of the chapter address this catalogue of variables.

Another approach to take is to compare the definition and conceptual sketch of African literature presented here with the definitional conceptualization by Ayuk (2014). While acknowledging the similarities between world litertures, he tries to list some common features of African literature. These are the pervasive use of proverbs and plot – abrupt exposition of conflict between man and man, man and society but rarely man and self. Others are character – the recurrent use of the concept of tragic hero, and some very common themes like nudity (where Africans believe distinctly that nudity begins and ends with genitals only), polygyny, time – the notion of African time, jungle justice, Christianity against animism, corruption, and colonialism.

5.2. Chinua Achebe versus Ngugi wa Thiong'o

But these definitions still leave room for a debate on which is the most appropriate language to use in African literature. Ngugi (1986) makes a convincing case for the use of only African languages in his major work, *Decolonizing the Mind*. He details the circumstances that led him from abandoning writing in English in favour of writing in his mother tongue, Gikuyu, and in the East African lingua franca, Swahili in 1977. He decries the fact that most African authors write in foreign languages – the language of the imperialists – languages that were relatively imposed on them. He is convinced that there is a need to create a literature that conveys the true African experience from the perspective of the local, not the visitor or outsider, and he has demonstrated this in many of his works (e.g. wa Thiong'o 1993, 2004, 2005, 2009, 2012, and 2016). He believes strongly that what African writers have created so far is a hybrid tradition that can only be termed Afro-European literature. He asserts "How we view ourselves/ our environment is very much dependent on where we stand in relationship to imperialism in its colonial and neo-colonial stages." (Ngugi 1986: 88).

Indeed, Ngugi has maintained these positions throughout the years as crystalized in a 2013 British Broadcasting Corporation (BBC) interview (HardTalk, July 2013: https://www.youtube.com/watch?v=A9iNMIG5TH8), where he even challenges that somehow surprising notion from some people that English is an African language as contained in the following exchange between the interviewer and Ngugi:

Q: You wrote very adequately in *Decolonizing the Mind* that [while] the bullet was the means of physical subjugation, language was a means of spiritual subjugation ... and that's part of the journey of your life to write not in English for your novels, but to write in Kikuyu. Why did you take that decision? You took it in prison, didn't you?

A: Language is so basic to any community. What I found is very interesting, whenever one people have colonialized another, they always impose their language, whether the French, the Portuguese, any...

Q: And you took ironically the decision while you were imprisoned by arap Moi after the colonial powers had left. That was a

Kenyan that put you in prison, because you were a dangerous writer.

A: The whole point about language is that after some time it will become what is called a metaphysical empire, the empire of the mind. Language is central to the whole idea of metaphysical empire. ... For me all languages are wonderful, be it Swahili, Kikuyu. But the problem has been, in a system of oppression and aggression, it's a hierarchy of power relationship between languages. Not which language is better, it's which language is higher than the other.

Q: I wondered, you know, the great African writer Chinua Achebe, he suggested that it wasn't quite the case as you put it, but also Ngozi Adichie, a younger Nigerian writer – she says, "English is my language". She's taken over it. I just wonder whether your views were very much of that time of the fifties and the sixties... and the younger African writers take a different view.

A: English is not an African Language. Full stop. One can say we adapted it, so on. In Nigeria there's Yoruba, Igbo, in Kenya there's Kikuyu, Luo. We have genuine African languages.

Q: But Chimamanda Ngozi Adichie says "English is mine. I've taken ownership with English". So she's kind of decolonized herself in a different way, hasn't she?

A: No. She's part of the metaphysical empire. Metaphysical empire is when people now begin to claim that this space is really mine. That doesn't mean that what she and my son Mukoma do with English isn't wonderful. But when we do that we're contributing to the expansion and deepening of the English language, not the Yoruba or Kikuyu or Kiswahili.

Q: You translate your own works into English. So, isn't that contributing?

A: No, translation is a very important process of how languages and cultures communicate. Look at the contribution of translations to the rise of European literature and languages.

It is very clear from the above sources that Ngugi wa Thiong'o excludes any writing in English, French, Portuguese, Chinese, Japanese and any other foreign language as being African literature.

Chinua Achebe, the author of one of the most famous novels to come out of Africa, *Things Fall Apart*, takes a completely different view from Ngugi wa Thiog'o. In a response to Ngugi's positions in *Decolonizing the Mind*, which Achebe considers as a criticism of him and other writers who write in European languages, Achebe (1989) in *Politics and Politicians of Language in African Literature* (this title itself being a literary indirection deployed against Ngugi since the sub-title of *Decolonizing the Mind* is 'the Politics of Language'') states:

"I write in English. English is a world language. But I do not write in English because it is a world language. My romance with the world is subsidiary to my involvement with Nigeria and Africa. Nigeria is a reality which I could not ignore." (Achebe 1989: 100)

From the above confrontation between Achebe and Ngugi we see that the vast majority of Africans speak one language and write in an entirely different language. This issue underlies what the Ivorian writer, Amadou Kourouma, terms as 'diplosie' (Kourouma 1991), the reality that the vast majority of African writers presumably think in one language and express themselves (speak or write) in another. The term 'diplosie' here may be a misspelling and/or mistranslation of the known linguistic term 'diglossia'. In any case, it looks as if we are in a dichotomous situation, an "either…or" situation where African literature is defined in terms of whether or not a piece of writing is truly African literature depending on its medium of expression. It seems this classical debate has come to a stalemate.

In this lecture, I wish to revive it with a relatively new perspective, bringing in contributions from proto-type theory as espoused in studies within Linguistics and Cognitive Science.

5.3. Contributions from Linguistics and Cognitive Science

In works within linguistic and the cognitive sciences (e.g., Rosch 1977, Wittgenstein 2001, and Taylor 2003), there is a growing trend whereby the classical, definitional approach to categorization within which something either absolutely belongs to a category or doesn't is less favoured to approaches where we think of a gradational approach to group membership. In this approach, some group members are more prototypical than others depending on the fact that they have more features of the group than others. We shall espouse this position with a number of illustrations and then use that to address the language question in African literature.

Categorization

Humans have the linguistic and cognitive abilities to categorize things in the world (Rosch 1977, Wittsgenstein 2001, Taylor 2003, Miyamoto 2013). We may categorize objects in the physical world such as tables, chairs, cars, dogs, cats; types of people such as teachers, friends, Black, White; and abstract categories such as theft (Miyamoto 2013).

We may do this by using the definitional approach to category membership, where a category would emphasize the set of all things that are joined together under a common label, and this definitional approach is established or determined by checking a list of all necessary and sufficient features (Miyamoto 2013) that account for the concept.

But as Rosch (1977), the linguist and cognitive scientist observes, the weakness to the definitional approach is that we are not told how we discover definitions and thus it does not explain important aspects of the processes of human categorization.

Prototype Theory of Categorization

Rosch (1977) instead proposes a prototype theory of categorization whereby categories have prototypes – category structure is created by the relationship between category members and the category prototype (Rosch 1977, Taylor 2003, Miyamoto 2013). A prototype to these scholars is a mental representation of a concept which retains the typical characteristics of many particular examples; and categorization decisions are based on the similarity of a specific instance to the prototype of a category (Rosch 1977, Taylor 2003, Miyamoto 2013). As Miyamoto (2013) indicates, the concept of a cat would be some animal that has the features as listed in Diagram 7; then any members of the cat family will have more or less the features indicated, with the prototypical members exhibiting more of these features.

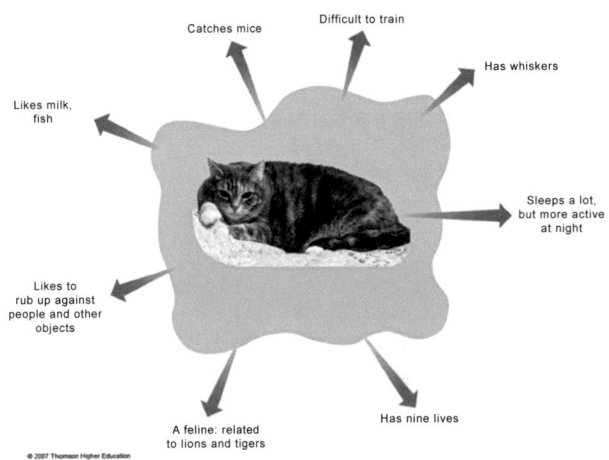

Diagram 7: Prototype Theory of Categorization
(Source: Psychology 355: Cognitive Psychology, Instructor:
John Miyamoto, 02/26/2013: Lecture 8-1)

Evidence for the prototype approach to categorization has been found from various semantic memory experiments within Cognitive Science. The idea is that subjects are faster to verify that prototypical objects are in the category than non-proto-typical objects (Rosch 1977, Taylor 2003, Miyamoto 2013). For instance, if one is asked to name prototypical categories of furniture in a room in an experiment, subjects are likely to mention *chair, table, stool, desk*, but hardly a *computer* or a wooden piece of artwork hanging on the wall (Bodomo 2013).

Prototype Experiment with List of Languages

With particular reference to our current topic, if people are asked to list African languages or identify the most proto-typical African languages in a list, *English, French,* and *Portuguese* will not be the first to be listed nor will they be high on the list, if at all they are listed.

We did a proto-type experiment involving the administration of questionnaires to 200 people of all ages and nationalities in Vienna and London between February 2014 and April 2014, with more than half being Africans (Bodomo 2014), asking them to identify a list of languages, either as being African or not being African. Here are the results:

Which of the following languages, in your opinion, are African languages?

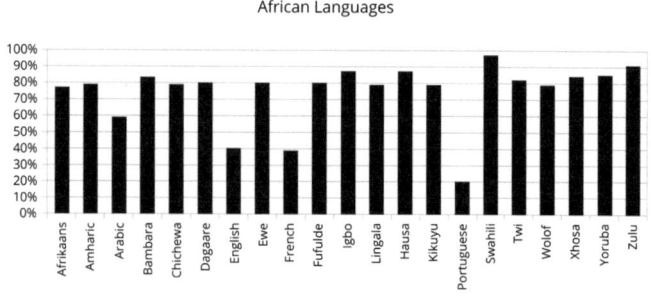

Diagram 8: African Languages

Which of the following languages, in your opinion, are NOT African languages?

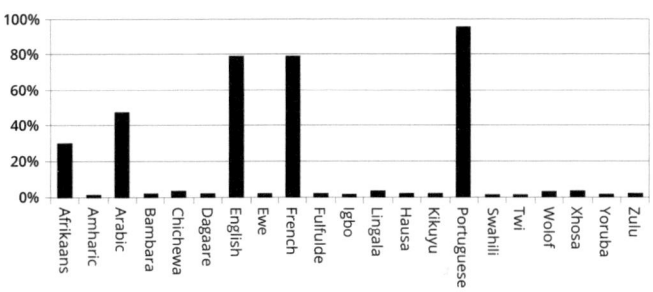

'Not' African Languages

Diagram 9: 'Not' African Languages

As can be seen, even though the former colonial languages are listed as African languages in diagram 3 (20% for Portuguese and 40% each for English and French) they have the lowest percentages when subjects were asked to identify items on the list that are African languages. This means that these former colonial languages, in line with the proto-type theory, are African languages but they are not proto-typical African languages.

This is further confirmed by the answers given when subjects are asked to identify members of a list of languages that are not African languages (diagram 4). The former colonial languages have the highest percentages (98% for Portuguese and 80% each for English and French), again suggesting that they are not proto-typical members in the category of African languages.

How does this discussion from prototype theory inform us about this classical debate about the definition of African literature with respect to the language of expression? The classical debate, as we have seen in the case of Achebe and Ngugi, has taken the form of a dichotomy, an "either … or" scenario. But this is contrary to proto-type theory which informs that we are better off taking a more gradational approach, a more nuanced, proto-typical approach to membership categorization. With this in mind, we may now redefine African literature in section 4.

5.4. Redefining African Literature: Pluralizing literature

In our working definition of African literature we came up with the following:

African literature is a form of artistic creation produced in the medium of any natural language (written or spoken) by an artist or group of artists with substantial enough experiences of the landscape of the continental landmass of Africa and its associated islands, along with diasporic exportations of the cultures of this continental landmass.

But as it is clear, though any language may be used as a medium of African literary production, those languages that are more able to express African cultures and African experiences of the continental landscape of Africa should be more prominent in expressing African literature. These languages should be more prototypical than the others, in line with proto-type theory.

Therefore, we may come up with the following diagram of African literatures and the language question where African languages occupy the centre:

African Literatures

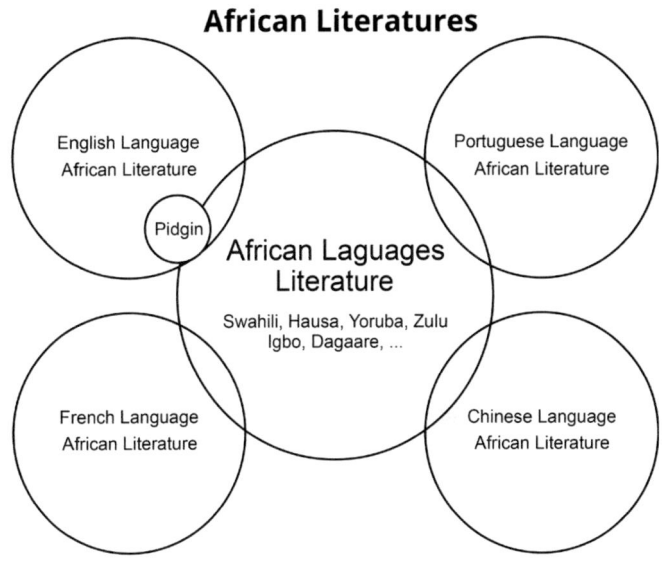

Diagram 10: African Literatures

In this approach, as illustrated in diagram 10, we do not necessarily exclude the idea that any language can be used to express African literature; rather, we express the idea that some languages are more natural, more prototypical in the expression of African literature and African culture in general than others. Hence, we have African language literature at the centre, these are the most proto-typical. Then comes other types of African literature: English language-based African literature (Anglophone African literature), French language-based African literature (Francophone African literature), and Portuguese language-based African literature (Lusophone African literature). In a rather hypothetical but predictive scenario in the near future, we can add Chinese language-based African literature (Sinophone African literature), given that there is now a huge number of Chinese speakers in Africa in the region of two million (Bodomo 2012, 2020, Bodomo and Pajancic 2016).

It is possible that pidgin-based forms of African literature may begin to emerge as shown on the diagram, and indeed, the works of the Nigerian writer Amos Tutuola in *The Palm Wine Drinkard*, is a typical example of this kind of literature. However, my prediction is that major indigenous African lingua franca like Swahili, Zulu, Yoruba, and Akan will develop very fast to eclipse Pidgin English and other pidgin-based European languages as lingua franca among the African masses, despite the attempt by neo-colonial broadcasting corporations like the British Broadcasting Corporation to promote Pidgin English in Africa.

In short, then, the consequences of this approach using proto-type theory is that we must now accept the fact that there are several types of African literature depending on which group of languages we use:

African language literatures
(Akan, Dagaare, Hausa, Igbo, Swahili, Yoruba, Zulu, etc literatures)

European language African literatures
(African literature in English, French, German, etc)

Asian language African literatures
(African literature in Chinese, Japanese, Hindi, Korean, etc)

This approach means that we can now afford to finally redefine African literature, putting African languages at the centre of the constellation:

> *African literature is any form of artistic creation produced in the medium of African languages, first and foremost, or any other natural language (spoken or written) by an artist or group of artists with substantial enough experiences of the landscape of the continental landmass of Africa and its associated islands, along with diasporic exportations of the cultures of this continental landmass.*

5.5. Conclusion: Towards a Pan-Africanist Agenda for African Literature in the Context of World Literature

In conclusion, we now have a pluralized agenda for African literature. We can no longer talk of African literature but African literatures. There are consequences for evolving such a pluralized agenda in terms of priorities.

Since resources are scarce, and we cannot continue to do any type of African literature in an unlimited way, the question of priority and prioritization now has to set in. Since, so far, we have shown by the application of prototype theory that, ceteris paribus, African languages are the prototypical and more natural media through which African literature should be produced, the only logical thing is to evolve a research agenda whereby African languages would be at the centre of African literary research.

Following this focus on African language literary research, we also need to reconceptualize the contribution of African literature in the general body of world literature. Borso (2017) tells us that literature often challenges us to reconceptualize many things in our society, including the "politics, economics, and sciences of life." As such, this reconceptualization of African literature allows us to argue that African literature has a new role to play not only in the general African society but in the way this reconceptualized literature contributes to world literature. In the past, world literature and comparative literature studies have often pointed to the works of African writers who write in the former colonial languages, English, French, and Portuguese. Hardly have we seen contributions of writers who write in African languages, with the exception of probably prominent ones like Ngugi wa Thiong'o. From now onwards, if the discussion from this chapter is to be taken seriously, any studies or compilation of world literature or comparative literature is incomplete without Afriphone literature as described above.

Africans of all walks of life and sympathetic Africanists must evolve an agency agenda to ensure that Afriphone literatures take hold in the 21st Century. This is the best way for African literature to contribute to world literature.[20] As a linguistic pan-Africanist strategy, African institutions ought to create a huge market for literature in African languages, for Afriphone literature, by encouraging and rewarding the writing of books in African languages.

---

[20] For African writers to be relevant in terms of their contribution to world literature from an Afriphone perspective, they must take steps to learn how to read and write in, at least, one African language.

CHAPTER 6

FROM AFRICA TO THE WORLD: AFRICAN LANGUAGES IN THE GLOBAL CONTEXT

6.1. Introduction

In this chapter, we look at how African languages can play a major role, not only in Africa, but in the world. At this point, I want to argue that the best way for Africa to influence the world – be it in diplomacy, literature, science, etc - is not through the medium of its former colonial languages, but the medium of its own languages. Africans must not storm into the world as anglophone Africans, francophone Africans, lusophone Africans but as AFRIPHONE Africans.

6.2. Linguistic pan-Africanism and Global Future

We have already defined and explained the concept of global future as any event that can bring seismic changes to the world at large. (Patomaki 2016). Roxburge et al (2020), as we saw earlier in chapter 1, is a major report on global future that stresses the importance of global climatic conservation in order that we can achieve prosperity. Examples of global futures – events and happenings that may have widespread effects on the world - include climate change, migration, robotics, space technology, and blockchains. If one were to manage these well, one could create opportunities for global inclusive economic growth. It is this current thinking that has led to the maxim 'our common future' – meaning that all human beings have a common future, have an interest in managing these current happenings that can have major impact on all of us, on a global future. The great advantage of this kind of thinking, of this kind futuristic thinking involving shifting our mindsets where problems and opportunities are assessed before they occur, is that we can take control of our destiny and look to the future with optimism.

However, given the current political, economic, and cultural asymmetries in the world, there is another view, led by scholars like Vijay Prashad (e.g. Prashad 2020), who argue that the idea of a common global future may indeed be rather idealistic and indeed goes to serve Western interests more than the interests of the Global South. We may, indeed, not have a common future with the West or Global North as a whole, as we, the people of the Global South, have not yet even secured our present. As Vijay argues, how can we be talking of our common future when we have not yet even secured our present in the Global South? (Prashad 2020). Without securing our survival there may not even be a future to share with those who have secured their present. You don't ask a hungry populace to cut down on its current consumption so as to save the climate to ensure a sustainable future.

I argue here that language policy, language preservation, in general, and linguistic pan-Africanism in particular, must be seen as an important aspect of our global future. So far the topic of language preservation and revitalization has not often featured much in issues of environmental conservation, and this is a great mistake. Linguists must make a clear link between the policy of language documentation, preservation, and revitalization as an important aspect of the global future phenomenon of climate and environmental preservation.

Linguistic pan-Africanism is an attempt to preserve, revitalise, and promote African languages as a way to secure Africa's present so that Africa can be prepared to take part in our common global future with other parts of the world.

Throughout this lecture, we have argued for the promotion of the use of African languages in all aspects of human transaction within Africa. We have proposed a model suggesting how this can be done within the education sector, within various regional co-operations, and even at continental level. In this section of the lecture, we outline a number of ways Africa and Africans can project African languages onto the world.

One aspect of the rise of nations and parts of the world is that they take their languages with them as they rise. Linguistic issues are an important part of the foreign policy of rising nations. For instance, the major countries of Europe have strong linguistic and cultural institutions that promote their languages globally. There is the Alliance Francaise, for instance, that teaches French and promotes French culture throughout the world. There is the Goethe Institute that is doing the same for German language and culture. And we have the British Council that promotes British culture and interests globally. With the rise of China there are now more than 200 Confucius Institutes throughout the world (Stambach and Kwayu 2017). Indeed in my own work on Africa – China relations (e.g. Bodomo 2010, 2017, 2020), I have indicated the growing importance of Confucius Institutes in Africa for promoting Chinese language and culture.

As Africa rises and as African voices become more prominent in the world, Africa must not showcase itself in the medium of only English, French, and Portuguese; that is, in the medium of its former colonial languages. Africa must go into the world in the medium of indigenous African languages. African culture and African soft power must be manifested in African languages.

The Mandela Institutes:

In several papers (e.g. Bodomo 2009, 2015), I have proposed the establishment of African cultural institutes worldwide that are run, not by foreigners, but by the AU and or the individual African polities. My proposal has been to call them Mandela Institutes, though of course we can reserve some of them for other Pan-African icons like Kwame Nkrumah, Thomas Sankara, Abdel Nasser, Mwalimu Julius Nyerere, or Tafawa Balewa.

These Mandela Institutes would be mandated to teach African languages and cultures worldwide with curricula designed by a coordinating body in Africa that produces curricula content for the teaching of these languages and the cultures associated with them.[21]

Standardized Tests in African Languages:

A coordinating committee for creating standards for testing proficiency levels must be established. A standardized test called Test of African Languages as a Foreign Language (TALaFoL) must be established. The curriculum should be the same for all African languages, such that, for instance, we can have TALaFoL Afirihili, TALaFoL Hausa, TALaFoL Yoruba, TALaFoL Igbo, TALaFoL Akan, TALaFoL Dagaare, TALaFoL Wolof, TALaFoL Zulu. Of course, it might also be possible to find an African name for the test so that we avoid using only the acronym

---

[21] There have been several reactions to the idea of the proposed Mandela Institutes. Some have asked, why just only Mandela? I have allowed room for other pan-African icons to also be named after these institutes. Others have also said that African does not have enough money to set up these institutes. My response is that, in the long run, these institutes can finance themselves. On the other hand, a reviewer for this publication is of the opinion that these institutes are more feasible than a continental language. My response is that I take this statement as just an opinion from the reviewer. They have already been many such opinions, and I am sure there will be many more such opinions…as I have argued throughout the lecture, many revolutionary ideas that were thought to be not feasible have come to take root. I am convinced that Afirihili will develop into a continental lingua franca. Btw, that is not the only proposal of this 100-page lecture, just to remind the reader.

TALaFoL. All foreigners who come to study or invest or live in Africa would be required to take this test, recording various levels of proficiency in the appropriate African language, ie depending on where in Africa they are residing. A requirement for obtaining a residence permit would be demonstrating a pass in these standardized tests.[22] No non-African institution should be allowed to create, standardize, and take part in determining these language tests. Funding should entirely be from Africa and its diaspora. We must reverse the trend where foreign bodies from places like Europe and China coming to invest in Africa create institutions for teaching us their languages to a situation in which we require them to learn our languages in order to ply their trade in Africa.

To sustain such standardized tests we must train teachers to teach them. In addition to their general teacher training, teachers of these standardized tests in African languages should also be trained through a certification programme for a Certificate of Teaching African Languages as Foreign Languages (CeTALFoL). Again, an African language name can be arrived at as a replacement for this name and its acronym.

African Diaspora to the Rescue:

I have had meetings with several AU bodies and advised them on several issues concerning the African diaspora. In one of these periodic African diaspora meetings, often facilitated by the AU, stakeholders must agree on a 5-year plan (say from 2025 to 2030) to encourage all second and subsequent generation African diaspora members to acquire a major African language by passing TALaFoL[Afirihili], TALaFoL[Hausa], TALaFol[Zulu}, and so on. This way, African languages would automatically become

---

[22] Just to specify this does not include people applying for visas to visit the Africa...the emphasis is on people who want to live and work there, as language tests in one form or another are required in many other countries outside Africa.

widespread all over the world. As someone who has advised the AU and facilitated such diaspora meetings, it is my wish that one day, before 2050 – long before the projected realization date of the AU's Agenda 2063 - we would be able to hold our meetings mainly in Afirihili. One of the best strategies for promoting African languages worldwide is when Africa gets its diaspora members speaking, reading, and writing African languages.

CHAPTER 7

CONCLUSION

7.1. Summary

Mr. Chairman, Fellows of the Academy, distinguished listeners, I have been talking to you in the past hour on my chosen topic, *Linguistic Pan-Africanism as a Global Future*. In this lecture, I have made some reflections on the language question in Africa in the 21st Century, and have sought to answer the following questions: how can Africa place itself linguistically to compete economically and culturally? What are the strategies for evolving and implementing effective pan-Africanist language policies to ensure that Africa has a bright global future?

I will now proceed to summarize the main issues and proposals that have been made in this lecture, and then attempt to look into the future – speculating on the future of linguistic pan-Africanism and the broader language question in a rising Africa.

For those who have seen this text before the lecture, the text has quickly evolved into a book of about 100 pages. So, I have appropriately divided it into seven 'chapters'. In chapter 1, I introduced the key terminologies of the topic - pan-Africanism, linguistic pan-Africanism, and global future. Next, I explained the main theme of the lecture which is that for Africa to assure itself of a sustainable future, it must make use of its own indigenous languages as languages of development and evolve key indigenous lingua franca or languages of wider communication, with the ultimate goal of producing a continental lingua franca. Chapter 2 was where I outlined my theoretical and methodological underpinnings. In Chapter 3, I outlined in some detail the notion of types of pan-Africanism and focused on developing a theoretical model of linguistic pan-Africanism. The model emphasized the primacy of the mother tongue or language of cultural identity, the importance of evolving indigenous lingua franca, and the need for all Africans to speak one major lingua franca by the year 2050.[23]

Chapters 4 and 5 are key parts of the lecture. In the former, I have given a detailed analysis of how the theoretical model of pan-Africanism might be illustrated with the language situation in the African country I know best, Ghana. The latter shows how the theory of linguistic pan-Africanism might play in a major debate on the language question in African literature. Chapter 6 outlined the strategies needed to promote African languages worldwide. In this chapter, chapter 7, we conclude the lecture by summarising the main issues, making some recommendations, and looking at what challenges there might be in implementing these recommendations.

7.2. Recommendations: Ten Tenets of Linguistic Pan-Africanism:

1. Secure the Base: Be literate in your language of identity - every African child should be given the opportunity to learn to speak, read, and write in their mother-tongue or L1 or any

---

[23] Questions are constantly raised about how feasible my proposal of a continental lingua franca is and whether Africa needs this at all as other continents don't have one lingua franca. Well, first of all, if we take North America as a continent, it has one lingua franca, English. Second, within pan-Africanism, Africa is not just seen as a continent but as a united political entity. The AU Agenda 2063's Aspiration 2, Goal 1 sees Africa as a Federal or Confederate United Africa. My proposal is that such a Federal or Confederate Africa requires a major lingua franca...the proposal doesn't say it should be the only lingua franca – we can have regional lingua franca as well. The issue is that Africa already has a supra continental lingua franca – English (French is not a supra lingua franca in Africa, compared to English)! Why kick against replacing this foreign lingua franca with Afirihili?

one of their languages of identity. This first tenet builds on wa Thiong'o's (2016) writing about the importance of the mother tongue and beyond.

2. Evolve linguistic pan-African policies: Current national language policies are both nationalistic and Eurocentric but not pan-African enough. For instance, one of the most important national language policies in Africa, the South African language policy (Kamwangamalu 2004, Wright 2004), evolved under Mandela's rule, recognizes 11 languages including indigenous South African languages, Afrikaans, and English but not a single language beyond southern Africa. Every African child must be given the opportunity to speak, read, and write in at least three languages: their language of identity, one African language, and Swahili (along with one international non-African language as an added bonus, not as a compulsory requirement).

3. Language of literary expression: Every African writer should, first and foremost, endeavour to write in his or her language of identity or any other African language.

4. Regional pan-African lingua franca: Every political/economic region of Africa: North, Southern, East, West, and Central Africa should evolve one to three regional lingua franca: For instance: Arabic in the North, Swahili and Amharic in the East, Zulu in the South, Lingala in Central Africa, and Hausa, Bambara, and Wolof in West Africa.

5. African languages in the service of Africa: Knowledge of an African language besides one's own is a requirement for serving in regional and continental level organizations.

6. Avoid petty nationalism and eurocentrism in national language policy: **All** national language policies attempt to be nationalistic. In reality, **most** are Eurocentric, and **few** are pan-Africanist in orientation. It is time to start seeing cross-regional language learning. For instance, East Africans learning West African

languages and vice versa, North Africans learning Southern African languages and vice versa.[24]

7. Generously fund the African language agenda: Regional and Continental level institutions and charity organizations and individual Africans should dedicate sections of their running costs to funding prizes and research grants for the promotion of African languages and literatures. Scholarship schemes, with funding from governments and charity organizations, should be set up for foreign students to learn African languages.

8. Language of the diaspora: All diaspora Africans should be encouraged to learn to speak, read, and write Swahili – and eventually Afirihili - as it has the greatest potential of becoming the most widespread pan-African language.

9. Afirihili: African linguists must work towards developing Swahili, the most widespread pan-African language into an official pan-African language called Afirihili, with a large segment of vocabularies from many African languages being part of the new language.

10. African languages in the world: All foreign students who come to study in Africa, most people seeking permanent residence permits in Africa, must be made to pass standardized tests in an African language.

7.3. Challenges:

In preparing this lecture, a colleague who read through a preliminary version of the work, asked why I am writing a 100-page lecture that no one will act on. He asked me if I trust the

---

[24] One of the cross-regional languages can be part of the trilingualism that I suggested but could also be in addition to it. This is especially feasible with scholars who may want to specialise as translators. The trilingualism proposal does say Africans should learn to speak, read, and write only three languages.

AU and African governments that much to waste my time? Well, my response is that as a scholar of African linguistics and literature and as an advocate for the promotion of the use of African languages, it is my duty, first, to contribute to the body of literature on how we can do this, and then, second, advocate and campaign for the AU and national and regional governments to act. Who knows what happens in the next five or 10 years? A new era may come in where new actors at the AU and within national and regional governments will be looking into the archives for solutions, for answers to the language in Africa.

Another challenge that has often been posed to me is whether I am not proposing an educational system in which children will learn too many languages. Well, it is not asking too much to propose a pan-Africanist language policy involving additive trilingualism in an already hyper-diverse and multilingual continent like Africa. The UN Decade for Indigenous Languages 2022 to 2023 should actually provide motivation to emphasizing Africa's indigenous languages. Many academic linguists have pointed to the rich diversity of African languages, language families and language types (e.g. Bamgbose 1991, 2014, Batibo 2005, Bresnan 1990, Chumbow 2009, Kamwangamalu 2009, Laitin 1994, Lauwo 2021, Mchombo 1997, Wolff 2016, etc). Such linguists quickly add that any attempt to try to homogenize and sanitize – so to speak – this linguistic diversity will lead to an educational system that would not resemble the African scenario. It would rather resemble colonial scenarios where all products of the African educational structure read and write more European languages than African languages. In any case, many Africans already speak three or more languages. So all we are asking is for them to learn to read and write in these languages.

A third challenge is on the issue of resources. A question is always asked: where do we get money to mount programmes in all these languages? I would say it is a question of priority. A lot of money has been spent in teaching Africans how to read and write in the former colonial languages throughout Africa. If only we could spend even half of what we spend teaching English, French, and Portuguese in teaching African languages, there would be enough resources to go around in implementing our linguistic pan-Africanist model of localized additive trilingualism.

Thank you, Barka, Akpe, Medaase, Nagode, Asante sana!

APPENDICES

A. Acknowledgements

I wish to acknowledge the following individuals and institutions without whom this lecture would not have been possible:

Akan translations:	Victoria Ofori, Kofi Agyekum
Dagaare translations:	Faustina Tantie, Mark Ali, Mary Bodomo, Dikpetey Sanortey
Hausa translations:	Ahmed Amfani, Li Chunguang
Swahili translations:	Mfilinge Nyalusi, Laurent Gabriel Ndijuye
Arabic translations:	Aziza Benlamoudi
Amharic translations:	Lemlem Fitwi
Academic comments and copy editing:	Mary Bodomo, Sam Mchombo, Paul Kerswill, Dong Hongjie, Eunice Wangui, Kofi Agyekum, Pius Babuna, and reviewers of the GAAS publications unit.
Lecture sponsorship:	The University of Education, Winneba for partial sponsorship of the inaugural lecture
Formatting and PowerPoint preparation:	Bettina Busch, Ulrike Auer
The University of Vienna:	for continuous funding of my professorship

GAAS officials, Helen Yitah, Kate Boampong

Biography of Prof Dr Vengvengnaa Bonlakyere Bodomo

Professor of African Studies
(with specializations in African Linguistics and Literatures, African
Diaspora Studies, and Africa – China – Europe Relations)

Adams Bodomo (born May 6, 1959) is a Ghanaian academic, who is a University Professor of African Studies (holding the Chair of African Languages and Literatures) at the University of Vienna, Austria – the first Black to occupy this top academic position in an Austrian university.

He has been Head of the University's Department of African Studies (2016 to 2018) and is Director of the Global African Diaspora Studies (GADS) Research Group at the University. Prof. Dr. Bodomo has done pioneering research in many disciplines including African linguistics, Afriphone literature, diaspora studies with a particular focus on diaspora community contributions to the socio-economic development of their countries of origin, Africa - China - Europe relations, and interdisciplinary studies across many humanities and social science disciplines.

Born in Jirapa Municipality, Ghana, Africa, Prof. Dr. Bodomo attended Nandom Secondary School (1973 to 1980) before attending the University of Ghana, Legon, Accra (1980 to 1987), where he earned a BA (Hons) in Linguistics, French, and Swahili, and an MA in Linguistics at the same university. He then moved to Norway where he earned MPhil and PhD degrees at the Norwegian University of Science and Technology (NTNU), Trondheim, Norway (1988 to 1997). Vengvengnaa Bodomo has taught at many universities around the world including the University of Ghana (1985–87), NTNU (1997), Stanford University (1994 - 1996; 2006 – 2007; and 2011), the University of Hong Kong (1997 to 2013), Bayreuth University (2012), and the University of Vienna (2013 to present).

Prof. Dr. Bodomo has won several prestigious fellowships and research projects. In 2011 he won a visiting fellowship to spend a semester at Stanford University's Humanities Center and in 2012, he was a fellow at Bayreuth University. He has won several research projects from the Hong Kong Research Grants Commission to do research on comparative African and Asian languages and cultures and to research the African presence in China.

Prof. Dr. Bodomo has written 20 books and more than 100 journal articles and book chapters. His most prominent books are (i) The Structure of Dagaare (CSLI, Stanford University, 1997), which is a pioneering study on the grammatical structure of his native language, Dagaare, spoken in northwestern Ghana and adjoining areas of Burkina Faso; and (ii) Computer-mediated Communication for Linguistics and Literacy (IGI Books, 2010). This is a pioneering study on the way languages and literatures are written and studied in the era of social media. Others are (iii) Africans in China (Cambria Press, 2012), the first book on the African migration and diasporization in China and other parts of Asia, which was shortlisted for the Africa - Asia book prize in 2015, and (iv) the globalization of foreign investment in Africa: the role of Europe, China and India (Emerald Publishing, 2018).

Prof. Dr. Bodomo has published in top journals. These include *Natural Language and Linguistic Theory* (on Dagaare serial verbs), *Linguistic Inquiry* (on Chinese classifiers), and *The China Quarterly* (on the African diaspora in China). Others are *World Economics* (an article that for the first time shows that African diaspora remittances to Africa are higher and more useful than ODA or official foreign aid) and *Lancet Public Health* (a short article on how Africans in China manage barriers to health care access).

He edits, has edited, or is on the editorial boards of many journals and books series, including the *Journal of West African Languages, Advances in Language and Literary Studies, Journal of African American Studies, Studies in African Linguistics,* and *African Language Grammars and Dictionaries.*

He belongs to several professional organizations including being life-time member of the African Studies Association (in America), the Linguistic Society of Hong Kong (in China), and the Federation Internationale de Langues et Literatures Modernes (FILLM) - a UNESCO affiliate, where he is President (2020 to 2023).

Professor Bodomo speaks or understands several languages including Dagaare (his native language), Twi, Swahili, English, French, Norwegian, German, and Chinese.

Beyond academics, Vengvengnaa Bodomo is an outdoor sports enthusiast (hiking and marathon-running – and now coach) and a poet. He mentors many young writers through founding and running literary clubs like the Vienna African Writers (VAW) club and charities like Yelmenga Foundation for the Humanities (YFH).

Professor Bodomo's fuller CV may be obtained from his University of Vienna homepage at:

https://homepage.univie.ac.at/adams.bodomo/

REFERENCES

Abdul-Raheem, T. (ed.). 1996. *Pan-Africanism: Politics, Economy and Social Change in the Twenty-first Century*. New York: New York University Press.

Adegbija, E. 1994. Language Attitudes in Sub-Saharan Africa: A Sociolinguistic Overview. Clevedon, Philadelphia and Adelaide: Multilingual Matters.

Agyekum, K. 2018. 'Linguistic imperialism and language decolonisation in Africa through documentation and preservation.' In Jason Kandybowicz, Travis Major, Harold Torrence& Phillip Duncan (eds.), African Linguistics in the prairie, pp 87-104. Berlin: Language Science Press. DOL 10: 5281/zenodo.1251718.

Akin Aina, T. 1993. Development Theory and Africa's lost decade. In: Changing Paradigms in Development - South, East and West, von Troil, Margareta (ed.).

Alexander, N. 2008. Creating the conditions for a counter-hegemonic strategy: African languages in the twenty-first century. in Globalization and language vitality: Perspectives from Africa, C.B. Vigouroux and S.S. Mufwene, 255-71. London: Continuum.

Ali, M. and Adams Bodomo. 2021. Ye Gorogor Yaa: Dagaare Folktales in Parallel Texts. LIT Verlag, Vienna, 241 pages.

Anyidoho, Kofi. 1992. Language & Development Strategy in Pan-African Literary Experience. Research in African Literatures, vol. 23, no. 1, 45–63. Indiana University Press. http://www.jstor.org/stable/3819948.

Arcand, J. L., Guillaumont, P., & Guillaumont Jeanneney, S. 2000. How to make a tragedy: on the alleged effect of ethnicity on growth. Journal of International Development: The Journal of the Development Studies Association, 12(7), 925-938.

Arcand, J. L., & Grin, F. 2013. Language in Economic Development: Is English Special and is Linguistic FragmentationBad?. English and development: Policy, pedagogy and globalization, 17, 243.

Asante, S. K. B. and D. Chanaiwa. 1993. 'Pan-Africanism and Regional Integration', in A. A. Mazrui and C. Wondji (eds), UNESCO General History of Africa, vol. 8. Berkeley: University of California Press, 724–743.

Attobrah, Kumi. 1972. *Ni Afrihili Oluga. The African Continental Language*. Pyka Press.

Asmara Declaration. 2000. Against All Odds: African languages and Literatures into the 21st Century. Asmara, Eritrea.

Ayuk, H. 2014. What is African literature? [Online] Available: http://princehamilton.blogspot.co.at/2009/06/what-is-african-literature.html (June 6, 2014).

Balakrishnan, Sarah. 2016. Pan-African Legacies, Afropolitan Futures. Transition 120, 29-37.

Bamgbose, Ayo. 1991. Language and the nation: The language question in sub-Saharan Africa, Edinburgh: Edinburgh University Press.

Bamgbose, Ayo. 2014. The language factor in development goals. Journal of Multilingual and Multicultural Development, 35(7), 646-657, DOI: 10.1080/01434632.2014.908888.

Bangura, A. K. 2012. Pan-Africanism: An Exploration of Afro-Asian Connections. CBACC Occasional Monograph, No. 25.

Bangura, A. K. 2000. Measurable effects of multilingualism in Africa. International Journal of the Sociology of Language, 146, 111-117.

Barker, P. 1986. Peoples, Languages and Religion in Northern Ghana. Ghana Accra: Evangelical Committee.

Batibo, H. 2005. Language decline and death in Africa: Causes, consequences and challenges, Clevedon: Multilingual Matters.

Baugh, J. 1994. The Law, Linguistics, and Educational reform for African American language minority students, ms Stanford University.

Bodomo, A.B. 1994. Language, History and Culture in Northern Ghana: An Introduction to the Mabia Linguistic Group. Nordic Journal of African Studies 3(2).

Bodomo, A. B. 1995. Multilingualism and its Challenge to Educational Planning in Ghana, ms. Stanford University.

Bodomo, A. B. 1996. Linguistics, education and politics: An interplay on the study of Ghanaian languages. Languages of the World, vol. 10. Lincom Europa, München, Germany.

Bodomo, A. 1996. On Language and Development in Africa: The Case of Ghana. Nordic Journal of African Studies 5 (2), 31–51.

Bodomo, A. B. 2009. Africa-China relations: symmetry, soft power, and South Africa. The China Review: An Interdisciplinary Journal on Greater China, Vol. 9, No. 2 (Fall 2009), 169-178.

Bodomo, A. B. 2012. Africans in China: A Socio-Cultural Study and its Implications on Africa-China Relations, Cambria Press, NY, USA.

Bodomo, A. 2013. Lecture Notes on Language, Literacy, and Literature: The language question in African literary expression, Department of African Studies (Course no 140251), University of Vienna.

Bodomo, A. 2014. Survey Report on African Languages and Literatures, Unpublished manuscript, University of Vienna, Austria.

Bodomo, A. B. 2015. African soft power in China, in: African – East African Affairs. 2015, 2, p. 76-97.

Bodomo, A. B. 2016. Afriphone literature as a prototypical form of African literature: Insights from prototype theory. In: *Advances in Language and Literary Studies*. 7, 5, p. 262-267.

Bodomo, A. 2017. African languages, linguistics, and literatures: exploring global interdisciplinary research trends in the humanities. Inaugural Lecture Monographs Series Vol. 1. Galda Verlag, Berlin, 50 pages.

Bodomo, A. 2017. The Globalization of Foreign Investment in Africa: The Role of Europe, China, and India, Emerald Publishing Limited, UK, 136 pages.

Bodomo, A. 2018. Tense and time-depth in the Mabia languages of West Africa: Testing the philosophy of linguistic relativity. Agwuele, A. & Bodomo, A. (eds.). *The Routledge Handbook of African Linguistics*. Abingdon/New York: Routledge, p. 438-449.

Bodomo, A. 2020. Identity packaging in Africa – China cross-cultural communication. In Tembe, Pausl and Vusi Gumede (eds) Cultures, Identities, and Ideologies in Africa – China Cooperation. Thabo Mbeki Institute and Africa World Press.

Bodomo, A. 2020. Historical and contemporary perspectives on inequalities and well-being of Africans in China, Asian Ethnicity DOI:10.1080/14631369.2020.1761246.

Bodomo, A. B. & Pajancic, C. 2016. Counting beans: Some empirical and methodological problems for calibrating the African presence in Greater China, in: *Africans in China. Guangdong and Beyond* (ed. Adams Bodomo), 2016. Diasporic Africa Press, New York. p. 139-155.

Bodomo A., Abubakari H. & Issah, S. 2020. Handbook of the Mabia Languages of West Africa. Galda Verlag, Berlin, Germany. 400 pages.

Bodomo, A.B. and Mugane, J. 1995. Language and development in sub-Saharan Africa. The case of Ghana and Kenya, ms. University of Trondheim, Norway and Stanford University, California.

Borso, Vittoria. 2017. "Bio-Politics and the Dynamic Multiciplity of Bíos: How Literature Challenges the Politics, Economics and Sciences of Life." Vortrag im Rahmen der internationalen Tagung "Biopoetics - Constructions of Life in Literature and Theory" an der Eötvös Loránd University Budapest, organisiert von der Association for General Studies of Literature, Budapest, 01.-02.06.2017.

Bresnan, Joan. 1990. African languages and syntactic theories. Studies in the Linguistic Sciences 20, 35-48.

Chumbow, B. S. 2009. Linguistic Diversity, Pluralism and National Development in Africa. Africa Development 34 (2), 21–45.

Davidson, B. 1994. The Search for Africa: A History in the Making. London: James Currey.

Degesys, Gediminas. 2014. Metamorphoses of Pan-Africanism Ideology in Researches of Civilization's and Cultural Identity. LOGOS-VILNIUS (78), 30-44.

Dolphyne, F.A. and Kropp-Dakubu, M.E. 1988. The Volta-Comoe Languages. In: The Languages of Ghana, M.E. Kropp-Dakubu (ed.).

Duthie, A. 1988. Ewe. In: The Languages of Ghana, M.E. Kropp-Dakubu (ed.).

Esedebe, O.P.P. 1982. Africanism: The Idea and the Movement, 1776–1963. Washington, DC: Howard University Press.

Fardon, R. and G. Furniss. 1994. African languages, development and the state. New York: Routledge.

Felix, Chinewe. 2002. Africa and the Challenges of Globalization: A Critical Appraisal of the Relevance of Pan-Africanism. Enugu State University of Science and Technology, Nigeria.

Fishman, J. A. 1966. Some contrasts between linguistically homogeneous and linguistically heterogeneous polities. Sociological inquiry, 36(2), 146-158.

Gerlach, L. 2016. N!aqriaxe – The Phonology of an endangered Language of Botswana. Wiesbaden: Harrassowitz Verlag

Goldsmith, John. 1990. *Autosegmental and metrical phonology.* Oxford: basil Blackwell.

Grin, F. 2005. Linguistic human rights as a source of policy guidelines: A critical assessment. Journal of Sociolinguistics, 9(3): 448–60.

Guevara, Raul Diaz. 2013. Pan-Africanism: A Contorted Delirium or a Pseudonationalist Paradigm? Revivalist Critique. Sage open 3(2).

Gyekye, K. 1997. Tradition and Modernity: Philosophical Reflections On The African Experience. New York and Oxford: Oxford University Press.

Harding-Esch & Coleman 2017. Language and the Sustainable Development Goals Selected proceedings of the 12th Language and Development Conference Dakar, Senegal, 2017.

Hegel, G. W. F. 1956. The Philosophy of History, trans. J. H. Clarke (New York: Dover).

Henderson, Brent. 2011. African languages and syntactic theory: impacts and directions. In Eyamba G. Bokamba et al. (eds.), Selected Proceedings of the 40th Annual Conference on African Linguistics, 15-25. Somerville, MA: Cascadilla Proceedings Project.

Hurskainen, A. 1993. Knowledge or Prejudice? Bridging the Communication Gap between Center and Periphery. Nordic Journal African Studies 2(2): 23-41.

Hurskainen, Arvi. 2004. Swahili language manager: a storehouse for developing multiple computational applications. Nordic Journal of African Studies 13 (3): 363 – 397.

Kamwangamalu, Nkonko M. 2004. The Language Planning Situation in South Africa. Language Planning and Policy in Africa, Vol. 1. Ed. Richard B. Baldauf Jr and Robert B. Kaplan. Great Britain: Cromwell Press Ltd., 197-281.

Kamwangamalu, Nkonko. 2009. Reflections on the language policy balance sheet in Africa. Language Matters, 40:2, 133-144, DOI: 10.1080/10228190903188567.

Kamwangamalu, Nkonko M. 2010. Vernacularization, globalization, and language economics in non-English-speaking countries in Africa. Language Problems and Language Planning 34(1), 1-23.

Kamwangamalu, Nkonko M. "The Language Planning Situation in South Africa." Language Planning and Policy in Africa, Vol. 1. Ed. Richard B. Baldauf Jr and Robert B. Kaplan. Great Britain: Cromwell Press Ltd., 2004. 197-281.

Kanneh, Kandiatu. 1998. African identities: Race, nation and culture in ethnography, Pan-Africanism and Black literatures. London: Routledge.

Kerswill, Paul & Edward Salifu Mahama. 2019. Ethnicity, conflict and language choice: the case of northern Ghana. In Matthew Evans, Lesley Jeffries & Jim O'Driscoll (eds.) *Routledge Handbook of Language in Conflict.* London: Routledge, pp. 339–360.

Khan, Mariama. 2014. Indigenous languages and Africa's development dilemma. Development in Practice 24 (5-6), 764-776.

Kodjo, E. and D. Chanaiwa. 1993. 'Pan-Africanism and Liberation', in A. Mazrui and C. Wondji (eds), UNESCO General History of Africa, vol. 8. Berkeley: University of California Press, 744–766.

Kourouma, A. 1991. Comments. In F. Osofisan, et al. (Eds.) Proceedings of the International Symposium on African Literatures, 2-7 May 1988, Lagos, Nigeria = Compte rendu du Colloque sur les litteratures africaines (pp. -). Lagos: Centre for Black and African Arts and Civilization.

Kropp-Dakubu, M.E. (ed.) 1988. The Languages of Ghana. KPI Ltd. London.

Ladefoged, Peter and Ian Maddieson. 1996. The Sounds of the World's Languages. Blackwell Publishers.

Laitin, D. 1994. The Tower of Babel as a Coordination Game: Political Linguistics in Ghana. American Political Science Review 88(3): 622-634.

Lauwo, Monica Shank. 2021. Literacies and translanguaging in Africa: A critical review of sociocultural perspectives, Southern African Linguistics and Applied Language Studies, 39(2), 210-224, DOI: 10.2989/16073614.2021.1934051.

Leben, W. R. 1973. Suprasegmental Phonology. M.I.T. dissertation. Garland Press, 1980.

Legere, Karsten. 2021. Linguistic identity in and out of Africa. In: Ilaria Micheli, Flavia Aiello, Maddalena Toscano, Amelia Pensabene (eds.) 2021. Language and Identity. Theories and experiences in lexicography and linguistic policies in a global world (ATrA, Aree di transizione linguistiche e culturali in Africa, vol.7), pp. 18-34 Trieste: EUT - Edizioni Università di Trieste, ISBN 978-88-5511-267-3 (print), ISBN 978-88-5511-268-0 (online).

Lewis, M. Paul, Gary F. Simons & Charles D. Fennig. 2009. Ethnologue: Languages of the world. Vol. 16. SIL international Dallas, TX.

Marinotti, J. P. 2016. Final Report: Symposium on Language and the Sustainable Development Goals New York, 21-22 April 2016.

Mazrui, A.A. and Mazrui, A.M. 1998. The Power of Babel: Language and Governance in the African Experience. London: James Currey Ltd.

Mazrui, A. A. 2000. 'Cultural Amnesia, Cultural Nostalgia and False Memory: Africa's Identity Crisis Revisited', African Philosophy 13 (2): 87–98.

Mchombo, Sam. 1997. Contributions of African languages to generative grammar. In Herbert, Robert K (ed.), African linguistics at the crossroads: papers from kwaluseni, 179-206. Koln: Rudiger Koppe Verlag.

Mchombo, Sam. 2017. Politics of Language Choice in African Education: The Case of Kenya and Malawi. International Relations and Diplomacy, vol 5, No 4, pages 181 – 204.

Miyamoto, J. 2013. Introduction to Categorization Theory. [Online] Available: https://faculty.washington.edu/jmiyamot/p355/lec08-1.p355.spr14.pdf (June 6, 2014).

Mudimbe, V.Y. 1988. The invention of Africa, Bloomington: Indiana University Press.

Mungwini, Pascah. 2017. Pan-Africanism and Epistemologies of the South. Theoria 64 (153), 165-186.

Mutere, Malaika. 2012. Towards an Africa-centered and pan-African theory of communication: Ubuntu and the oral-aesthetic perspective. South African Journal for Communication Theory and Research 38(2), 147-163. https://doi-org.uaccess.univie.ac.at/10.1080/02500167.2012.717345.

Nantambu, K. 1998. 'Pan-Africanism versus Pan-African Nationalism: An Afrocentric Analysis', Journal of Black Studies 28, no. 5 (May): 561–574.

Ndhlovu, Finex. 2008. Language and African Development: Theoretical Reflections on the Place of Languages in African Studies. Nordic journal of African studies 17 (2), 137-151.

Ndhlovu, F. 2009. The Limitations of Language and Nationality as Prime markers of African Diaspora Identities in the State of Victoria. African Identities 7(1): 17–32.

Ndlovu-Gatsheni, Sabelo J. 2015. Decoloniality as the Future of Africa. History Compass 13(10), 485-496.

Nkrumah, K. 1964. Consciencism: Philosophy and Ideology for Decolonization and Development with Particular Reference to the African Revolution. New York: Modern Reader Paperbacks.

Nyamnjoh, F. B. and K. Shoro. 2010. 'Language, Mobility, African Writers and Pan-Africanism', African Communication Research 4(1): 35–62.

Nyawalo, Mich, 2017. Afro-futurism and the aesthetica of hope in Bekolo's Les.

Onwudiwe, Ebere, and Minabere Ibelema (eds.) 2002. Afro-Optimism: Perspectives on Africa's Advances. Praeger.

Organization of African Unity [OAU] 1986. Language plan of action for Africa. http://www.acalan.org/an/ouaplan.htm (accessed April 19, 2021).

Ouane, Adama. 2014. Vers un nouvel humanisme : la perspective africaine. Int Rev Educ 60, 379–389. https://doi-org.uaccess.univie.ac.at/10.1007/s11159-013-9396-7.

Patomaki, Heikki. 2016. Global Futures. Wiley Online Library. Available from: https://www.researchgate.net/publication/314465054_Global_futures [accessed Oct 27 2021].

Patomaki, Heikki. 2019. Repurposing the university in the 21st century: toward a progressive global vision. Globalizations 16 (5), 751-762. https://doi-org.uaccess.univie.ac.at/10.1080/14747731.2019.1578533.

Pattanayak, Debi. 1990. Multilingualism in India. Multilingual Matters, 136 pages.

Phaahla, P. 2010. Multilingualism in a global village: What is the future of a local language (e.g. Northern Sotho) in an increasingly globalized world? South African Journal of African Languages, 30:1, 52-65, DOI: 10.1080/02572117.2010.10587335.

Pondi, J. 1987. The OAU: From Political to Economic Pan-Africanism. SAIS Review 7(1), 199-212. doi:10.1353/sais.1987.0057.

Prah, K. 1993. Mother-Tongue for Scientific and Technological Development in Africa. German Foundation for International Development.

Prah, K.K. 1995. African languages for the mass education of Africans. Bonn: Education, Science and Documentation Center.

Prah, K.K. and H. Ochwada (ed.). 2005. 'Historians, Nationalism and Pan-Africanism: Myths and Realities', in T. Mkandawire (ed.), African Intellectuals: Rethinking Politics, Language, Gender and Development. Senegal: CODESRIA, 201.

Prah, K.K., 2011. 'The language of development and the development of language in contemporary Africa: The challenge of African development in the context of current linguistic realities and dominant knowledge in applied linguistics'. Paper presented at the Annual Conference of the American Association for Applied Linguistics (AAAL), Chicago, Illinois.

Prashad, Vijay. 2020. *Washington Bullets*. LeftWord Books.

Ramose, M. B. 1991. 'Self-determination in Decolonisation', in W. Twining (ed.), Issues of Self-determination. Aberdeen: Aberdeen University Press, 25–32.

Ramose, M. B. 1999. African Philosophy through Ubuntu. Harare: Mond Books.

Ramose, M. B. 2015. 'On the Contested Meaning of Philosophy', South African Journal of Philosophy 34 (4): 551–558.

Rickford, J. 1995. Language, education and cultural diversity. In: Migration in Europe: Challenges and Opportunities (The Stanford Berlin Symposium on Transition in Europe), H. Donenbachen, K. Kramer and S. Baughman (eds.), pp. 70 -84. Berlin: Stanford Program in Berlin.

Rosch, E. 1977. Classification of Real-World Objects: Origins and Representations in Cognition. In P.N. Johnson-Laird, & P.C. Wason (Eds.), Thinking: Readings in Cognitive Science (pp. 212–222). Cambridge: University Press.

Roxburgh, T., Ellis, K., Johnson, J.A., Baldos, U.L., Hertel, T., Nootenboom, C., and Polasky, S. 2020. Global Futures: Assessing the global economic impacts of environmental change to support policy-making. Summary report, January 2020. https://www.wwf.org.uk/globalfutures.

Sapir, E. 1929. The Status of Linguistics as a Science. Language, vol. 5: 207-219.

de Saussure, F. (1916) 1959. Course in General Linguistics. New York: McGraw-Hill.

Sesanti, Simphiwe. 2017. Pan-African Linguistic and Cultural Unity. A Basis For pan-Africanism and the African Renaissance. Theoria 64(153), 10-21. https://doi-org.uaccess.univie.ac.at/10.3167/th.2017.6415303.

Shepperson, G. 1962. Pan-Africanism and "Pan-Africanism": Some Historical Notes. Phylon (1960-), 23(4), 346–358. https://doi.org/10.2307/274158.

Shivji, I. 2011. 'The Struggle to Covert Nationalism to Pan-Africanism: Taking Stock of 50 Years of Africanism', Keynote Address to the 4th European Conference on African Studies, Uppsala, 15–18 June.

Sibanda, O. 2021. The Advent of the African Continental Free Trade Agreement as a Tool for Development. Foreign Trade Review, 56(2), 216–224. https://doi.org/10.1177/0015732521995171.

Simala , I.K. 2002 . Empowering indigenous African languages for sustainable development. in Speaking African: African languages for education and development, F. Owino, 45-53. Cape Town: The Centre for Advanced Studies of African Society.

Simala, I. K. 2003. Pan-Africanism and the Language Question: Re-reading African Cultural and Intellectual History. African Journal of International Affairs, vol 6 nos 1 and 2, pp 19 – 53.

Soske, Jon. 2015. The impossible concept: Settler liberalism, Pan-Africanism, and the language of non-racialism. African Historical Review 47 (2), 1-36. DOI10.1080/17532523.2015.11 30188.

Stambach, Amy and Aikande Kwayu. 2017. Confucius Institutes in Africa, or How the Educational Spirit in Africa is Re-Rationalised Towards the East, Journal of Southern African Studies, 43:2, 411-424, DOI: 10.1080/03057070.2017.1298290.

Taylor, J. R. 2003. *Linguistic Categorization.* Oxford: University Press.

von Troil, M. (ed.) 1993. Changing Paradigms in Development - South, East and West. The Scandinavian Institute of African Studies.

Trudell, Barbara. 2009. Local-language literacy and sustainable development in Africa. *International Journal of Educational Development* 29 (1), 73-79.

Trudell, Barbara. 2010. Language, culture, development and politics: dimensions of local agency in language development in Africa, *Journal of Multilingual and Multicultural Development,* 31:4, 403-419, DOI: 10.1080/01434632.2010.497216.

Ugwuanyi, Lawrence Ogbo. 2017. Critiquing Sub-Saharan Pan-Africanism through an Appraisal of Postcolonial African Modernity. Theoria 63(153), 58-84. https://doi.org/10.3167/th.2017.6415305.

Wa Thiong'o, N. 1986. Decolonising the Mind: The Politics of Language in African Literature. Oxford, Nairobi, Portsmouth: James Currey, EAEP, Heinemann.

Wa Thiong'o, N. 1993. Moving the Centre: The Struggle for Cultural Freedoms. Oxford, Nairobi, Portsmouth: James Currey, EAEP, Heinemann.

Wa Thiong'o, N. 2004. African Identities: Pan-Africanism in the Era of Globalization and Capitalist Fundamentalism. Macalester International 14, Article 9. Available at: http://digitalcommons.macalester.edu/macintl/vol14/iss1/9.

Wa Thiong'o, N. 2005. 'Europhone or African Memory: The Challenge of Pan-Africanist Intellectual in the Era of Globalization', in T. Mkandawire (ed.), African Intellectuals: Rethinking Politics, Language, Gender and Development. Senegal: CODESRIA, 162.

Wa Thiong'o, N. 2009. Something Torn and New: An African Renaissance. New York: Basic Civitas Books.

Wa Thiong'o, N. 2012. 'Remembering Africa: Memory, Restoration and African Renaissance', in H. Lauer and K. Anyidoho (eds), Reclaiming the Human Sciences and Humanities through African Perspectives, vol. 2. Accra: Sub-Saharan Publishers, 1519–1535.

Wa Thiong'o, N. 2016. Secure the Base. London, New York, Calcutta: Seagull Books.

Walters, R. W. 1993. Pan-Africanism in the African Diaspora: An Analysis of Modern Afrocentric Political Movements. Detroit, MI: Wayne State University Press.

Webb, V. and Kembo-Sure. 2000. African voices. Oxford: Oxford University Press.

Weitzberg, Keren. 2019. Living with Nkrumahism: Nation, State, and Pan-Africanism in Ghana. Canadian Journal of History-Annales Canadiennes D Histoire 54(1-2), 238-240.

Wiredu, K. 1980. Philosophy and an African culture. Cambridge: Cambridge University Press.

Wiredu, K. 1996. Cultural Universals and Particulars. Bloomington: Indiana University Press.

Wiredu, K. 1998. 'Toward Decolonising African Philosophy and Religion', African Studies Quarterly 1 (4): 17–46.

Wiredu, K. 2002. 'The Moral Foundations of an African Culture', in P. H. Coetzee and A. P. J. Roux (eds), Philosophy from Africa. Oxford: Oxford University Press, 287–296.

Wittgenstein, L. 2001. Philosophical Investigations (3rd ed.). Oxford: Blackwell.

Wolff, H. Ekkehard. 2016. Language and development in Africa: perceptions, ideologies and challenges. Cambridge University Press.

Woamck, Ytasha. 2013. *Afrofuturism: The World of Black Sci-Fi and Fantasy Culture.* Chicago, Illinois: Lawrence Hills Books.

Wright, L. 2004. Language and value: Towards accepting a richer linguistic ecology for South Africa. Language Problems and Language Planning, 28(2): 175–197.

Zack-Williams, Alfred. 2016. Pan-Africanism and Communism: The Communist International, Africa and the diaspora, 1919–1939, Review of African Political Economy, 43(150), 681-684, DOI: 10.1080/03056244.2016.1249707.

Zeleza P. T. 2002. 'The Politics of Historical and Social Science Research in Africa'. Journal of Southern African Studies 28 (1): 9–23.

Zizwe Poe, D. 2003. Kwame Nkrumah's Contribution to Pan-Africanism: An Afrocentric Analysis. London: Routeledge.

INDEX